Unitarian Universalists of Color

Stories of Struggle, Courage, Love and Faith

Edited by Yuri Yamamoto, Chandra Snell, and Tim Hanami

Karen, Thank you for you

love, Yuri

Table of Contents

Listen
Listen to my story
So you may know me better... better... better

I am sharing a story
Of my own choice

For this brief moment
I ask you to suspend your own voice

And with no judgment, assumptions, or distractions
Let my story seep into your heart

When the time comes for you to speak
I will do my part

To listen
Listen to your story
So I may know you better... better... better

Listen
Listen to our stories
So we may know us better... better... better

Listen... listen... listen

Listen by Yuri Yamamoto
https://youtu.be/9OmYlwTqkP0

Foreword

We have all known the long loneliness, and we
have found that the answer is community.

Dorothy Day, Catholic activist

In spring 2013, a group of Unitarian Universalists (UU) religious professionals of color wondered aloud, "What would Unitarian Universalist faith development by and for UUs of color look like?" I decided to take this question to the people in the pews. An invitation to an online meeting was distributed through the congregational monthly mailing, on various email lists, and on uua.org. During the online meeting, a small group of people of different ethnicities representing the global majority reflected upon what they would like to experience in faith development resources.

Primary among their suggestions was the ability to gather with other UUs of color. I became determined to find a way to offer community to those who responded: to a young adult who has only recently discovered Unitarian Universalism in Idaho and who is the only person of color in their congregation, to a small group forming a diversity team in North Carolina, to an African American seminarian in California making decisions about where to focus their ministry, to a congregational leader who is not comfortable discussing with fellow congregants the microaggressions in their New Jersey congregation, to a multiethnic individual in Florida who finds it too painful to attend the local congregation.

Together, we created the Virtual Community of UUs of Color. We started with monthly meetings, where participants could join on the telephone or through their computer. We hear each other's voices, and with webcams and free video conferencing platforms, we see each other's faces. Some participants are regular, attending almost every month; others have the desire to attend, but find it hard to find the time. To keep the community connected between calls, I created a Google group where community members share about their experiences, turn to each other for support, and post announcements and links to resources.

People join the community by emailing me directly at jyork@uua.org. Though I attempt to keep the community safe by allowing only those who identify as UUs of color to join, members are free to share as they like in meetings and in the group, as long as it is done respectfully. The community is not perfect. Yet it attempts to fill a void in the lives of some Unitarian Universalists. The support of the Unitarian Universalist Association is crucial to the survival of this virtual community, and I am proud as a Unitarian Universalist to say that we have that support.

In the past two years, over one hundred individuals have asked to join the group. Sometimes there are two people in the monthly meeting, sometimes twelve. Even when attendance is low, community members consistently ask me to keep holding meetings: for some people, this is a lifeline to our faith. Members have taken the initiative to call meetings of UUs of color in their own congregations, districts, and regions. They have met at General Assembly. They have presented workshops and found new ways to engage with our faith. Some of them even came up with the idea of writing the book you now hold in your hands.

When the community was first launched, someone asked me, "How can people with different ethnicities and experiences support each other? After all, your experience as a black person will not be the same as mine or even the same as another black person's?" I wish that person participated in the community today. They would experience the value in having a community they can turn to, a place to share a story about being ignored in a committee meeting and having people *believe* them.

They would experience members conversing in Spanish and participants of Japanese heritage celebrating meeting another Unitarian Universalist of Japanese heritage for the first time. They would also experience our respectful disagreements and varied opinions. (As this book attests, Unitarian Universalists of color have different opinions and feelings about what it means to be a person of color in an overwhelmingly white association.) They would know of our gentle urgings to stand strong in the face of adversity.

Community—where values are tested again and again—is where faith development happens. It can happen in a religious education workshop. It can happen at a small group ministry session. And, yes, it can happen online with individuals from across the country who you may never meet face-to-face. It happens when we are asked to live our values faithfully in the world, thereby deepening our commitment to Unitarian Universalism made flesh as an active force in the world.

Jessica York
Faith Development Director,
Unitarian Universalist
Association

Preface

Many Unitarian Universalist congregations have little diversity when it comes to race and ethnicity. How does it feel to be a person of color in a predominantly white, liberal religious community? In the fall of 2013, three of us started this project to find out.

The project has led us to conversations, planning, reflections, fundraising, a panel workshop, and many new connections. It has been an amazing journey!

Are you a person of color wanting to connect with other Unitarian Universalists of color? Are you a member of a Unitarian Universalist community or another organization that is trying to become more multicultural? Do you simply love to read ordinary peoples' life experiences? Whoever you are, however you arrived here, we are thrilled to make connections with you now.

In this book, you will meet fifteen Unitarian Universalists of color who come from all walks of life, live in different parts of the United States, and are uniquely talented and beautiful. As such, each story is written in each writer's authentic style.

Some of us have known Unitarian Universalism for decades, and some of us have discovered this faith recently. Some of us love our congregations. Some of us have conflicting feelings. Some of us do not belong to any congregation at this time. Some of us play leadership roles, and some of us feel invisible.

We are proud to be unique individuals of color. Even though we share some experiences and traits with each other, we don't want to be defined only by the color of our skin.

We present these stories to initiate more conversations because Unitarian Universalism is our chosen faith, but the Unitarian Universalist community has not always been welcoming to people who look like us. What can our congregations do to become more welcoming? What can we do together to become more whole?

We invite you to see unique beauties in each story. Look beyond our styles, vocabularies and grammars to see how we chose to tell our stories. Imagine a conversation with us.

When individuals or congregations in the stories make you feel uncomfortable, we encourage you to reflect on and have a conversation about where the feeling may be coming from and the cultures and practices of your own congregation.

Unitarian Universalists are called by our first principle to affirm inherent worth and dignity of every person. Accepting that we all make mistakes, figuring out what to do when mistakes happen, and learning from the experiences are all essential aspects of the first principle.

We believe that every person, regardless of color, has a story worth sharing. Sharing stories is an important part of creating a community that celebrates authentic people. We hope that our stories will inspire you to reach out to others and start sharing your own stories. And we definitely look forward to hearing from you!

Welcome to our worlds! Now let us begin our journey together.

> With love,
> Yuri, Chandra, and Tim
> (https://UUofColorStoryProject.com/)
> January 2017

Acknowledgments

Numerous people helped make this book possible. Without Jessica York who started the Google Group for Unitarian Universalists of Color and all contributors who took time and risk to write their stories, this book would not exist. We greatly appreciate those who contributed to our Faithify campaigns to raise funds for the panel discussion at the Unitarian Universalist Association General Assembly in Portland, Oregon, in 2015 and for the publication of the book. The Diverse Revolutionary Unitarian Universalist Multicultural Ministries has been our inspiration and also hosted our workshop and promoted our fundraising campaigns. We also thank the Unitarian Universalist Fellowship of Raleigh for hosting the Faithify campaigns and donating a special Sunday service collection to the project. Finally, we thank our Unitarian Universalist friends who encouraged us along the way.

Introduction

This book consists of two sections.

The first section contains stories by fifteen Unitarian Universalists of color, two of whom wish to remain anonymous. Stories are presented roughly in the order of the length of our relationships with Unitarian Universalism.

This section also contains Eavesdropping pages interspersed throughout, featuring anonymous comments we have heard from other Unitarian Universalists of color in conversations or email. Identifying information has been removed from these comments, and some have been constructed from multiple comments about similar experiences.

The second section contains the edited transcript of a panel workshop at the Unitarian Universalist Association General Assembly in 2015. Revs. Jonipher Kwong, Carlton Elliot Smith, and Sunshine Wolfe were the panelists along with the coeditors.

A list of resources for further reading about people of color and Unitarian Universalism as well as anti-racism and multiculturalism is included in the appendix.

Section 1

Stories of Unitarian Universalists of Color

A Unitarian Universalist Diversity Story

Christopher Cameron

I first learned about Unitarian Universalism through my academic research. I am a history professor at the University of North Carolina at Charlotte; and after completing my first book, I was searching for a new research project. I had always been interested in eighteenth-century Deism and decided to start looking into its rise in early America. While doing so, I discovered that liberal religion was in many ways similar to Deism, and for some was even a midway point in their conversion from orthodox Christianity. This was especially true because liberal sects such as the Unitarians and Universalists felt it was necessary to adapt their theological beliefs to the findings of modern science and the Enlightenment. After discovering this close relationship between liberal religion and Deism, I decided to broaden the focus of my study to liberal religion in general.

At the same time, around early 2013, I was becoming more interested and involved in the freethought movement. I discovered groups such as African Americans for Humanism and Black Atheists of America and became aware of the strong presence of black freethinkers on blogs and social media. This piqued my personal interest because I consider myself an atheist and am African American. But it also piqued my scholarly interest because I had not read much about black atheism in the studies of African American religion.

After doing more research, I found that many black (and white) atheists still consider themselves religious and feel comfortable attending groups such as the Ethical Culture Society and the Unitarian Universalist denomination. This led me to check out the Piedmont Unitarian Universalist Church of Charlotte sometime in the spring of 2013.

I initially went to only two or three services at PUUC. I enjoyed the sermons, none of which mentioned God or posited belief in Jesus as necessary to living an ethical life. But I had received a fellowship to conduct research for a liberal religion project in Boston for a year, so I moved to Massachusetts in July 2013. If I had not received this fellowship, I am not sure whether I would have become a regular attendee or member of the church. While the sermons were nice and the people were welcoming, I found that most members were older white men and women. While these individuals did all they could to make my wife and me feel welcome, it was hard to feel at home in a setting where we were twenty years younger than most people and where there were few, if any, blacks attending the church.

In Massachusetts, I lived in a small town named Woburn, roughly fifteen miles north of Boston. There was certainly no lack of UU churches in the area, given that both denominations had their origins in eighteenth-century theological disputes in churches in the region. But when I went to the UU church in Reading, just outside of Woburn, I encountered a similar dynamic as I had experienced in Charlotte. There was no ethnic or racial diversity in the church, and most members were older. Also, during the summer, it appeared that Unitarian Universalists tend to travel quite a bit, so the church had few attendees. We went to two services during that first summer, and maybe one more in the fall, but that was it.

One thing I feel I should mention is that neither my wife nor I ever experienced discrimination of any sort in the church, whether overt or subtle. There was just a feeling that the church was not for us. It is hard to feel at home in a place where you simply feel that you are very different from everybody there. I could not see myself socializing with most of the members outside of church, because we did not have a lot in common. I come from a very impoverished, inner-city background and sometimes find it hard to relate to wealthier whites, even if we share the same educational level.

When we returned to Charlotte in July 2014, we began attending PUUC again sporadically, as well as the UU church in South Charlotte. Of the two, we definitely prefer the one in South Charlotte. The preacher is a bit more dynamic in his delivery, something that is important in African American culture, as most blacks in the United States have been raised in evangelical denominations that emphasize powerful and dynamic preaching. The one in South Charlotte is also a bigger congregation and has quite a bit of young people, even though there are still few African Americans.

So while we still don't feel entirely comfortable in a UU church, two major elements have pushed us to keep coming back, even if we do not attend regularly. The first is the heavy emphasis on social justice that is characteristic of all UU churches we have attended. I am a strong believer that any church, whether theist or atheist in its theology, should focus strongly on improving people's lives in this world. This seems to be one of the major functions and emphases of the UU church, so I really appreciate that.

From food drives to protests against police brutality against blacks to helping immigrants find employment to prison ministry, both churches in Charlotte seem to be incredibly active in a number of social justice causes that I believe in. I am especially interested in prison ministry, as I served eight months in a New Hampshire county jail on a drug charge starting when I was seventeen years old. This experience, and the fact that I was able to turn my life around and become a history professor, makes the work that UUs do with prisoners of great interest and importance to me.

The second major aspect of the UU church that continues to draw me in is its theological liberalism. I've had conversations with UUs that spanned the range from Deists to theists to agnostics to humanists and even pantheists. All theological views appear to be welcomed and embraced within the denomination. This is what drew me to the church in the first place, and it is what makes me continue to try to find community and fellowship within the UU church.

I can say that I would probably be much more inclined to join one of the UU churches in Charlotte if there were a greater population of young black people in the churches. This is due partly to my wife's preferences and partly to my own. While she also agrees with the theology and social justice mission of the UU church, she is still a bit hesitant to join an organization with seemingly so little diversity. And this hesitance on her part has influenced me. Were she pushing to attend a UU church regularly and become a member, I would likely also do the same, but her apathy sort of rubs off on me, so we often find some excuse not to attend Sunday services.

At the same time, we have attended only the early services at each church, so we will experiment with the later ones to see if we feel a different vibe there. I am hopeful that we will and look forward to the possibility of getting more involved, as I really love the principles and humanist focus of Unitarian Universalism.

From Christianity to Atheism: An Evolution of a Japanese American

Tim Hanami

Why am I an atheist member of the Unitarian Universalist denomination? This question bugged me for nearly a year as I left the Free Methodist denomination after being raised from birth to the age of twenty-one in a Japanese American congregation. Why did I leave what the Japanese call *kazoku,* or family, to worship on Sunday mornings with a bunch of white folks I really don't know? I guess the best thing to do is to start from the beginning.

I was born and raised in Los Angeles, a city that is diverse in culture and history. There are people of many different ethnic backgrounds, and that diversity was something I took for granted, something I always thought was normal. My church was in Los Angeles' Boyle Heights. Before the war, there were Jewish and Russian with pockets of Japanese immigrants and Mexican American. This structure eventually changed over the years to become the heart of East LA, which is more than 95 percent Latino. Yet I was dedicated to God by the late pastor, just after I was born.

So every Sunday, I went from infancy to junior high learning about the Bible, the love of Christ, and God's grace. But this was more than just Sunday school or church; it was a gathering of families one day a week to socialize and to feel the presence of love and family. Because of *kazoku*, we held everyone accountable. We helped one another during happy times as well as crises. This was more than just worshipping; this familial event guided us, shaped us, formed us, and kept us in check.

One thing about the Japanese and Japanese American culture of my church was that the Bible verse Matthew 6:14—"For if you forgive others their trespasses, your heavenly Father will also forgive you"— really did not apply, because if you lost face or shamed the family, you were ostracized.

So I was brought up not to bring disgrace to my family or myself. There was more culture involved than the Bible itself, and I felt comfortable with that lifestyle. Our congregation, the Pacific Coast Japanese Free Methodist Conference, differed from the white conference. Our ethnic enclave allowed us to praise God while keeping our culture. Whenever the president of the Free Methodist denomination or his representative visited our church, we would give him the red-carpet treatment, but when he left, there was a sigh of relief, because our private space was ours again. Well, that's how I felt—and probably many of the other members did too.

As I grew up in the church, I did the usual thing a church member would do. After becoming a member, I taught Sunday school (catechism/religious education) and did missionary work in Mexico to share the love of God with the poor Mexicans.

Prior to becoming a member, I had to attend classes, which lasted about a month and were taught by the lead pastor; these involved the church's history, beliefs, and so on. Just prior to becoming a part of the family, at age seventeen, I was so filled with the Spirit of God that I begged my pastor to allow me to join the membership class, because I wanted to share my dedication to God in front of the hundreds of members. I was finally allowed to take the class, and when it was over, I was asked to step forward with friends. My smiling pastor told me to get on my knees, and he poured anointed water on my head and blessed me in the name of the Father and Son and Holy Spirit.

I felt proud. I had given my life to God, and I was willing to travel around the world to preach the good news, as the Bible said: "And he said unto them, 'Go ye into all the world, and preach the gospel to every creature'" (Mark 16:15). I was part of the many disciples of Jesus. I was elated. I continued my mission work and taught Sunday school and was a camp counselor. So, from ages seventeen to nineteen, I shared God's love with youth.

Then something happened. I discovered the band Rush in 1983, and their talent amazed me. So I listened to Rush starting in 1983 as an alternative to Mötley Crüe and Ozzy Osbourne. I then turned from their 1983 release, *Signals,* to their first album in 1974. They rocked. As a former piano student, I was amazed by the complex rhythms as well as the lyrics. I then bought their next album, *Grace Under Pressure,* in 1984. I enjoyed the melody as well as the lyrics and memorized the whole album catalog from 1974 to 1984. I was enthralled, a captive audience, and I managed to attend one of their concerts in 1985. I was a Rush fan for life.

But something captured my attention in the lyrics of "Manhattan Project" in *Power Windows*: "Imagine a man when it all began/The pilot of *Enola Gay* flying out of the shockwave on that August day/ All the powers that be, and the course of history/Would be changed forevermore."

What was that August day? What was *Enola Gay*? I asked a friend who knew the answer and told me to go visit my Asian American Studies professor. She sat me down and explained everything. This was all a shock to me. My aunt, who died of cancer six months after 9/11, was a victim of the Manhattan Project in Hiroshima. I realized that the Allies who bombed a city of civilians—twice—were God-fearing Christians. The nails in the coffin of belief were being pounded shut.

Then, at age twenty-one, I found out that a family member was a victim of racism and was tortured by Christians because he looked like the enemy. As an eight-year-old, he was kicked and punched while being called Jap and Little Tojo.

This really got me mad, but the pièce de résistance was an article in the Free Methodist magazine in which white readers said that the Japanese American concentration camps were justifiable because they didn't know who the enemies were. Forget the fact that Japanese American men fought against the Nazis in Europe and Africa and managed to break the Japanese code, helping the United States end the war in Japan. The hatred some fifty years later was still lingering, so I left the church.

I realized that the faith I believed in was based on hatred. That racism against Japanese Americans was okay, though the denomination I worshipped in prohibits racism. The denomination takes pride in their antislavery stance but feared that my relatives were going to kill them after the attack on Pearl Harbor. What happened to Psalm 23:4: "Yea, though I walk through the valley of the shadow of death, I will fear no evil: for thou art with me; thy rod and thy staff they comfort me"? I wanted nothing to do with that racist environment ever again.

I also found out that many Japanese and Japanese Americans became Christians out of fear. Was Christianity based on fear and hatred? If it wasn't, there sure seems to be a lot of hatred from evangelicals. So I stopped going to church. I realized that if I did believe in God, it would all be a lie. I couldn't love something or worship in a place based on lies and racism, so I left the church and left my *kazoku*.

My heart was ripped apart. The love I'd had and the spirituality I'd felt died. There was a void inside me that would not heal. I decided that I could do something else, something to fill that void. So I became an atheist and got involved in the civil rights movement. I became a member of an Asian American club on my college campus, and I eventually became president and worked to promote Asian Americans.

From there, I delved into broader student activism by becoming a member of APSU (Asians and Pacific Islander Student Union). As Asian American activists, we fought for educational rights, attempting to end the model minority myth, and fought for civil rights for Asian Americans after Vincent Chin was murdered by two white men. Then the group blossomed into an organization that supported and marched with African American, Native American, Chicano, and white students.

We marched to our state capital for education rights, we protested Desert Storm, we supported reparations for more than sixty thousand Japanese and Japanese Americans, and participated in other progressive actions that would affect all people of color. I fought for labor rights, justice for janitors, women's rights, and LGBTIQ rights—and kept on fighting. I even taught folks in college about the struggles of being an Asian American.

Yet through all that, I still had Christianity inside me. Instead of using drugs to get away, I just went deeper and deeper into activism work. I wanted to rid myself of the cancer I felt and become normal.

Bible verses kept running through my mind as I tried hard to get rid of what I call the blemish in my life. As time progressed, I met fellow liberal atheists/spiritualists. Many of them were recovering Christians, and we chatted. We would use Skype and converse about our ideas. The chat eventually became an anti-Christian group. I made fun of Christians who did stupid and/or illegal acts, and I would post scripture showing their hypocrisy.

I felt after much research that Christianity was a religion of a conservative white-dominated culture. The white patriarchal emphasis was exposed to me as clear as day. Learning from my Asian American Studies class that Christianity and all its subsets made up only 1 percent of Japan's total population proved to me that this was not the faith for me.

Christianity was a faith that you either believe or you're dead. That is what was running through my mind. My heart was hardened, my feelings of hatred toward Christians regardless of political or social belief was strong, and I felt that Christianity went counter to everything within my culture.

Whether it was the "God hates f—s" group or the rapture-ready folks, I would post comments and Bible verses showing their hypocrisy. I used to get into flaming wars (text battles) on liberal sites when right-wingers tried to take over the conversation. Atheists on the left would cheer me on, and I would go nonstop—that is, until one day a liberal Christian took me to task. This Christian told me not to generalize all Christians as their right-wing counterparts.

This actually made me mad. Who were these Christians to tell me this? They even called themselves liberals. So I challenged them and threw Bible verses at them, but they returned fire. Eventually, I gave in and said, "Forget it. It's a waste of time."

Still, their liberalism was interesting. Their intellect was appealing, and I stopped calling the liberal Christians sheep and insulting their Jesus by calling Him Jeebus. I found their dedication and their fight for justice pretty neat, and they were also people of color. Yet I remained an atheist.

In 2012, after a night of chatting with friends on Skype and a night of right-wing-Christian bashing, a fellow atheist named Robert told me, "Why not check out the Unitarian Universalists?" I said, "Huh?" He explained to me the core values of the UU, and I said, "I'm an atheist." He told me that there are atheists in that church as well as Jews, Muslims, Buddhists, Sikhs, and other religious types—including animists, agnostics, and pagans.

This really confused me. I told Robert that I believed in science and not the Sky-Spook. He said that didn't matter. So for a year, I asked questions and came to realize that Robert was not a full atheist.

As a scientist, he said, "We can't prove a negative."

I said, "But there is no God."

"Prove it," he replied.

"Are you an atheist and don't believe that God exists?"

"As a scientist, I can't prove God either existed or did not exist."

This left me stumped.

So, after a year of discussion, I visited a Unitarian Universalist website and shot off an email to the pastor. Much to my surprise, Rev. Tera Little of Throop UU Church in Pasadena, California, responded. She explained what UU was, the history of the church, its programs, and so forth. Much to my surprise, everything Robert said was true. I also mentioned that I was an atheist, and the pastor did not care.

So, two weeks into the email conversation, I drove to the church. I stopped and then drove past. I was not ready to go into a church. The façade was beautiful, and the organic garden complemented the structure. But I went home. I was not ready. Then as 2012 came to a close and February 2013 approached, I decided on February 17 that I would go to church. I drove into the parking lot, parked and locked my car, walked in to the narthex, and saw a short woman with a stole.

That woman was Pastor Little. She said, "Tim?" I smiled and said yes, and she hugged me. This was kind of a shocker, as I was not used to this much love from a stranger. Regardless, I spoke to Pastor Little and thanked her.

Then the service started. It reminded me of church, and I felt kind of strange, but I continued on with the program and listened. I was amazed that there were no mentions of God or Jesus or the Holy Spirit. The service was about love, justice, and peace.

Then came the after-service lunch. I grabbed a plate, saying hello to others and thanking them for inviting me. I also told them how I found the church on the Internet. After I received my meal, I sat down by myself. Everyone was chatting and eating, and the pastor did not pray.

I said to myself, *I like this,* and I said under my breath, *"Itadakimasu,"* which in Japanese means "Thank you for the meal." In Japan, you thank the farmers for growing the food.

Soon some members, including the pastor, sat with me. Again more questions were asked, and I answered them. I also mentioned that I was an atheist. I was expecting the members to shun me or treat me with disgust, but a few of them said, "So am I!" I had thought that this was going to be a short visit, but I was with people like me. I also liked that there were some people of color. I had found my new church.

Then, on my birthday, which fell on a Sunday, I became a member and signed my name in the book. I was so happy. There was no baptism with water or a month-long class—just a brief conversation with my pastor. I was proud that day, because, as I said at the book signing, I was born twice—once on my birthday and again as a new member of the Unitarian Universalist family.

My life did change, but I still had issues with my past. My pastor recommended *Faitheist* by Chris Stedman. Stedman grew up as an evangelical, until he realized he was gay and turned into an angry atheist. He eventually created a successful interfaith group that incorporated religious and nonreligious folks to end hatred.

After reading his story, my life changed. I was no longer the angry atheist who tried to insult Christians; I knew love was a better plan than anger. I started to feel the love and no longer had anger about my past. The book allowed me to see that not all Christians are racists, patriarchal, or crazed but can be caring and loving.

I've come to realize that my anger made my life miserable, and blaming others only made my life more unbearable. I also learned about true love and forgiveness when I read about the shooting at the UU church in Tennessee on July 27, 2008. The members forgave the shooter, and the church seemed to be healing. No anger, no revenge—and the members chose not to seek the death penalty.

There was something more to the UU denomination. We work for civil rights and justice. I was encouraged to start an inquiry into the shooting death of a young, unarmed black man by the Pasadena Police Department. Though not sponsored by the church, we were offered access to the church facility and have been working to ask why he was killed.

I then was encouraged by my pastor to check out DRUUMM (Diverse and Revolutionary Unitarian Universalist Multicultural Ministries). When I did, I thought, *This is amazing—a group recognized by the denomination with basically a no-holds-barred look into UUs and people of color.* This really got me excited. As a person of color, what my previous church ignored, the UU addressed.

Then my pastor told me of a three-day conference in San Diego, which I attended. This event addressed people of color, our roles in the church, and how to attract more people of color into the churches and promotion of diversity. This event was something I always wanted, because my previous church was for only Japanese American. The Free Methodist denomination is divided into different ethnic conferences, and each conference has its own congregation. There are the Chinese, Mexican, Japanese conferences. The denomination felt that by segregating the congregations and creating separate conferences, people would feel more comfortable. So when I visited Throop Church, there was more than just one ethnic group under one umbrella. Yes, there are bilingual programs, but everyone is under the same building.

Though this seems ideal to me, and I feel that my UU church is more diverse than my previous one, the event in San Diego exposed challenges that need to be addressed, such as the planning of Sunday worship services, sensitivity issues, civil rights, and so on. The conference attendees felt that these issues must be addressed to prevent division.

Even as accepting and diverse as my church is, probably because Pasadena is a pretty diverse city, we still have our issues. During a book reading of *The New Jim Crow*, a white member brought up white privilege and managed to make another white member upset. I kept my mouth shut and listened. I just chuckled in my mind because what the member thought was an offense to them was the norm to people of color. Even the poorest white person has more rights than a wealthy person of color. There is also the privilege of being seen as an individual. Being an individual gives you the privilege of not being stereotyped.

I once heard something like this on a progressive radio station:

> Say that a white person is in line and berates the cashier in a supermarket. When the customer leaves and the next person who comes up is white, the cashier would most likely think, *What a moron*, and just continue helping the new customer. On the other hand, if the person berating the cashier is black and the customer behind the jerk is black, more likely than not, the cashier may think, *Oh no, what's next?*

My church tends to be open-minded, but there is still room for growth. The discomfort I saw in my church may be a warning sign, but blatant racism—be it intentional or unintentional—is not present in my church. Yet is it not present because they are truly open-minded or is it out of fear of offending me that they keep it to themselves? I am committed to help UU churches become anti-racist and more diverse.

I see potential in the UU denomination to address these issues from the revelation within DRUUMM. I am excited by DRUUMM, which is inclusive of all people of color. As a Japanese American, I sometimes feel like Asian Americans' stories are not well represented in Unitarian Universalism. Many injustices have been done to Asian Americans besides the Japanese concentration camps during World War II. I think that the model minority myth has kept these facts invisible, and whenever I think discussion becomes too focused on black and white in UU or wherever, I remind them about the oppressions my people have experienced. I actually was profiled and harassed many times by the local police department during the height of Asian American gang busting. I support Black Lives Matter because I know exactly how it feels to be targeted and brutalized by the police.

DRUUMM has inspired me to worship with fellow UUs and to continue my struggle to end racism as well as fight for racial equity. I believe that it can happen and that true change can happen, affecting the church, the neighborhood, and then our nation. As a relatively new member of a UU church, I see a bright future and hope.

Eavesdropping—1

I came to our church dinner a few times, and no one sat with me.
People who had already been there invited their
friends to their tables, but not me.
After that, I had to reassess my relationship with the church.

Whaddup: The Tr1umphant Story

Mike Jenkins

"Whaddup?"

English translation: "What's up?" or, more specifically, "What's going on?"

Most of the world knows me more comfortably as Mike Jenkins, but by the time this conversation is over, you will know me as "Tr1umphant"—emcee, hip-hop artist, survivor, scholar of the "School of Hard Knocks", and one of the very few Unitarian Universalists of color that you'll probably ever know. That said, take a seat. Lend me your ears and hear your own voice read these words through your mind. Sacrifice your eyes to the black-and-white truth of my life. Class starts ... now.

I was born in Detroit, Michigan, at 6:00 a.m., in the year 1980, at Hutzel Hospital. I was jaundice, and somewhat underweight. Because of that, I didn't go home for the first eight and a half weeks of my life. Raised by nurses and fed through a glass box, the first few weeks of my life were supported by rubber hands and, unfortunately, did not involve true human touch. I didn't experience nursing, like most infants, or being pressed to my mother's bosom to be burped, for that matter. But what I did have was music. And not just any music—the greatest music ever uttered on this old wet rock 360 light-seconds away from the sun. I experienced "The Motown Sound."

From Smokey Robinson to the Temptations, from Marvin Gaye to Stevie Wonder, I had it all—presented to me in the form of a somewhat large, metallic machine that was planted on top of my glass box every day. I stared at that thing as if it were my own personal singing sun that woke me up every morning and lullabied me to sleep every night like a serenading moon.

There was only one problem; Mommy didn't like that. One day, when my mommy came to the hospital to meet me in the nursery, my singing sun was on—shining above me. I turned to meet my mommy's eyes, only to see her in an escalated mood. She was yelling at the nurse that placed the metallic machine over me, thinking it affected the other apparatuses in the room to my detriment.

I was told that the nurse then yelled back, commanding my mommy to watch and listen to what's going on in this room, and she did. What she found was truly amazing to her. Mommy saw me...smiling. She saw me staring at my singing sun and smiling, my feet seemingly being tickled by the sound of the group "Earth, Wind, and Fire." My laugh was rhythmic. The scene was priceless. The sound was magnanimous. And the words, they stuck with me—even to this very day: "Music is my inspiration. Music is my life."

From those lyrics onward, my mommy was sold on the idea of that song being my anthem. Who knew how true it would be? Who knew that, by 1982, I would be diagnosed as a child with signs of Asperger's? Who knew that, by 1983, doctors and speech therapists would be assigned to me, only to alert Mom that I would have to be considered a "special needs child"? Who knew that, by 1985, both she and I would prove them all wrong? Who knew that, by 1989, I would be reading at the ninth-grade level, excelling exponentially in comprehension?

Who knew that, when nothing else worked and everyone else gave up on compelling me to speak, Mom would teach me to sing? Yeah, that's right. Every single lesson I learned from Mom was a song. My name, my address, saying and spelling "Mommy" and "Daddy," reading books, mathematics, you name it—that is how she taught me to learn. It's been a part of me ever since. Mom was my first musical idol. She was my emcee.

Mom was many other things, too. She was a Flower Power hippy girl who married an expat gone Black Panther, gone narcotics cop. She was a graduate of the University of Detroit in the field of psychology, and a social worker. She was also my first teacher of spirituality.

I was raised in a Pantheist home. Pretty much, we'd "put the lime in the coconut, and mix it all up." Buddha and Shiva salt-and-pepper shakers sat side by side. Chinese Jesus sat atop our living-room mantle. Sculptures of elephants representing Ganesh trampled their imaginary path across our marble coffee table. We lit candles like we were Catholic, schmoozed like we were Jewish, honored the lives of Muslims, decorated our house according to Feng Shui, and lit incense daily to respect many deities. The house, when it wasn't permeated with the scent of sweet cinnamon, was surrounded with sage. Oh, and by the way, Mommy practiced Santeria. So yeah, it was that kind of party.

Everything was great until about the fifth grade. That was when I stepped away from the blackboard and started to look around at other people, other things. That was when I realized that I was "different." That was when I was told that I was going to Hell because of being *that* kind of different. Before that moment, I had no idea what Hell even was. By age ten and a half, I was condemning my mom and dad verbally. Yeah, no kidding. Imagine that, if you will. A ten year old telling you that Jesus is the only way, and because you don't believe that, you are going to burn in Hell.

My teenage years were a melted, jaded blur of dark colors. I was bullied to the point of near exhaustion with a life I yet even lived. I had begun to rebel against all who loved me while succumbing to all who didn't. My only refuge...was hip-hop. Tupac Shakur, Notorious B.I.G., Onyx, and AZ were just my speed—an angry grade of poetic. It was my self-proclaimed, new voice. "Music Is My Life" got traded for "Betta Off

Dead." The Onyx's *All We Got Iz Us* LP featured an intro on the first track of two people—one coercing the other to shoot himself in the head. Like a ritual, I would push Play, close my eyes, and meditate to this—every morning.

My relationship with my mother? Diminished. My father and I began to clash more and more. My life as I wanted to know it seemed over. But then, out of what seemed to be nowhere, something happened to me that changed everything. His name...was Robert Plant.

One day, while scavenging through my dad's old stuff, which he'd cram in junk drawers, I came across a cassette tape. It was a Maxell, ninety-minute audiocassette that was at the halfway mark according to the black strip. It had a thin, celadon sticker on it that carried a phrase that, even to this day, haunts me deliciously in my harmonic dreams. It read "Stairway to Heaven."

I sneaked it into my pocket as if I had discovered something too taboo to ask about, and took it to my room. I placed my headphones into the audio jack, closed my eyes, and pressed Play. What I heard next changed my life—forever.

> There's a lady who's sure all that glitters is gold
> And she's buying a stairway to heaven.
> When she gets there she knows, if the stores are all closed
> With a word she can get what she came for
> Ooh, ooh, and she's buying a stairway to heaven...

By the time I got to "bustle in your hedgerow," I was already...in tears. By the solo? I had seen the last seventeen years of my life flash before my eyes in sync with the sound. More tears. And by the last, haunting fade of Robert Plant's voice as he sang his last words, I had become a Pantheist all over again. I must have played that album nine times that night in its entirety. I refused to sleep. I was in need of that revival—and revive I surely did. But just like the lady that Robert Plant was singing about, I wanted...to be sure.

The next sixteen years went by in a blink. Nine moves in eight states—from Michigan, to Alabama, to Florida, back to Michigan, to California, to New York, to Maryland, to Texas, to North Carolina. Four women—one who threw me away in six months' time, one who lost her mind, one who ripped my heart to pieces, and the one I'm married to now that put me back together. From having the *Leave It to Beaver*, wife-two-kids-and-a-dog, picket-fence life to homelessness. From alcohol, food, and drug addiction with suicidal tendencies to self-appointed "anger management" classes and cutting cold turkey— literally (I am now a vegetarian). From getting kicked out of the Christian church for telling the congregations all their rituals are Pagan, to getting booted from the Atheist community for "believing in myself," and everything in between—I'd been everywhere. Or so, I thought.

One day, while living miserably in Houston, my wife, Sabrina, and I had a conversation. Literally, we'd had enough. Had enough of being ostracized by the "traditional southern folk"—including everyone in her family—for being "our kind of different." Had enough of not being understood and accepted, let alone embraced, by a community of some sort that we could call family. Had enough of having enough, and we were going to end the madness starting at that very moment.

So, we began to do what most "new agers" do—we Googled. We YouTubed. We searched articles from *USA Today* to the *Wall Street Journal*. We looked to find a place where we could move that would give us the fulfillment we needed in order to flourish as we believed we should. The recurring answer...was Raleigh, North Carolina. And so we packed, and twenty-five hours later, with our whole lives in the back seat of our car, we were on Capitol Boulevard.

While at an extended-stay hotel, complete with altars dedicated to Kwan Yin and Moloch—our deities of choice at the time—we began to utilize Wi-Fi to our advantage. We began to search for a community of people of like minds. What we found...was UUFR—the Unitarian Universalist Fellowship of Raleigh.

That Sunday, we attended a service. Assistant Minister Karla Brockie led the service, which was for Dia de los Muertos. It had a Japanese bone dance. It was indeed "our kind of different." We liked it, yet we looked around throughout the hour, only to notice one thing: we were seemingly the only people of color there. And guess what? Believe it or not, it was exactly what we wanted! After all of the ridicule we'd received from people of color in the Baptist church and Messianic synagogues for our spiritual choice of pragmatic application, we were so happy not to see *anyone* who looked like us. Our individual pasts held us as anomalies in a crowded room full of Christian dogmatic reason—at least that's how both my wife and I have felt about our lives. It's an oxymoron that's just as painful to type as it is to read silently.

What sealed the deal for us was not the service itself (though it was presented well) or the sermon (though the points were, from where we stood, thought-provoking). It was coffee hour. We donned our blue tags, heading toward the "Blue Tag Express" line, not knowing exactly what to expect. Honestly, I thought we wouldn't get spoken to, because we were new. My wife thought we would just grab a small bite to eat from whatever pastries were available and just head home. We had *no idea* that we would be not only spoken to but embraced by this community—*forty-five times*. Yes, in total (and I counted), my wife and me were hugged by forty-five people. Complete strangers had shown us more love in forty-five minutes than we had felt from our entire families in the forty-five months we'd been together. I had transferred all of our banking information, shut off all utilities, set up storage units, and even begun looking for employment...by ten thirty the following morning.

What ensued after that was, to put it lightly, unbelievable. Being that my wife and me moved from Houston on a whim, we weren't prepared for the reality in Raleigh. We went out on faith that we would find work and housing before our savings ran out. Well? We didn't. Yeah, that's right. Job interviews abounded, without any of them giving much bite. Creative approaches toward prolonging our rent-a-week extended-stay suite were running out. I hoped for the best, but prepared for the worst.

Early one morning, I woke up with a gut feeling—a premonition that I couldn't possibly ignore. I feared that we were going to be kicked out that day. So, without any hesitation, my wife and I gathered our whole lives all over again and placed them in the backseat of our car. We then got dressed and went on multiple interviews throughout the day—to no avail.

We came back to the front door of our suite and, with a glimmer of hope, slid our keycard into the door. What we saw was devastating: a red light instead of a green one. The management had deactivated the keycards to our suite. We were officially kicked out and were forced to realize a haunting happenstance that I thought I'd never have to experience again—homelessness. No money, no job, no family—only the people we'd met at UUFR.

The minutes felt like hours. All of a sudden, I felt myself breaking inside. I felt like I was being violently awakened from the greatest dream, only to be force-fed a nightmare that I had prepared from scratch.

Strangely, my wife was...calm. And I mean *unbelievably*...calm. We drove to Lake Wheeler Park, delved into the outside for a while, took silly pictures, and shared scary silences. And then she called the minister. I, with my pride, couldn't do it—but she could, and she did. She reached out to UUFR for help. I thought it was a terrible idea. After all, I didn't want to be a burden to anyone. But she took my pride...and swallowed it for me.

And lo and behold, it actually worked. The congregation was willing to help us. Us—visitors of UUFR, complete strangers otherwise. Within hours, Karla Brockie had spoken with a couple that helped us. The next thing I knew, I was in a hotel room paid for by someone I had never met—for two full weeks. Within those two weeks, we managed to get jobs. And on the fifteenth day, one of the members of the congregation opened their doors to us.

We stayed in their home for close to *five whole months*. Each week, we mingled with more people. We even came across a man by the name of

P.K. Knotts—a person of color with a vigor for multicultural diversity the likes of which I had never seen before. By the end of the month, we had met and knew at least fifty people by name, exchanged phone numbers and stories about what brought us to UU, and even helped other new members feel welcome the way everyone did us.

I had even gained some intrigue from members after mentioning my passion for poetry and music, and I was approached by the music director and staff to offer it to the congregation—all this while being given the chance to save enough money to get ourselves on our feet and find a home.

In the month of March, that home found us. By mid-month, I was exchanging a check for the keys...to our new home. I *couldn't* believe it. If someone else had told me, I probably wouldn't have believed it. But it's true. The love of strangers *happened* to us. And now? They aren't strangers anymore.

In a service entitled "Who am I, where did I come from, where am I going?" I was one of three people who were presenting their story—the Music Director being one of them. My story, however, had a twist to it.

You see, I had no intention of presenting myself in any way other than true-to-life, so I made it a point not just to say my piece—but *sing* it. Part of my presentation was a rap. It had been years since I performed any of my work, but I was taking a chance to truly show myself. I felt nervous about the performance, but not the presentation—as this place felt better than family. I remember the statement I made, right before the music began: "I'm not a rock star, but I stay on tour."

And then, the beat dropped. "I'm an inhabitant of Tamu-rae-gaia, but more specifically/A michi-gala-bama-tampa-bay-area-cali-for-new -yorker-by-way-of-the-vintage-anna-poly-texan-north-carolinean lineage/Earth, Wind, Water, Fire, the elements/all one-hundred and nineteen of 'em/ to know me is to love me/to hug me is to touch them/ the grand anatomy of both she and him/bangin' into coexistence loud enough for you to feel me."

The song continued with rhymes ablaze. By the time I got to the end, there wasn't a single seat in the house that was perched upon, and all I could hear was a resounding round of applause.

"To my mom, I'm a bum/to my ex, I was sex and then done/to my people, I'm an indigenous sun/ And in the unforgiving minute, I'm sixty seconds run/ I'm as quiet as a riot, and intention's the pun/ MAKE SOME NOISE!"

And 'make noise'...they *did*. Everyone made a point to tell me how much of a gift my performance was to the congregation and how much it intrigued them to learn more about "being a rapper." I was shocked. I mean, think about it. How many places can you go to on a Sunday morning and perform Hip-Hop in a room full of people who've probably never given the genre more than three seconds worth of thought, only for them to enjoy it so much that they beg you to do it again and again?

To be able to express myself in this way and be loved for it—in a UU congregation, no less—is an absolute gift. Before I knew it, I had joined everything I could get my hands on. From musical performances with other musicians to the worship support team to the CUUPS Pagan group to even the Lay Worship Leaders group, which met with the minister himself, Rev. John Saxon, on a monthly basis to receive copious amounts of support regarding input toward the evolution of Universalism both within and beyond UUFR walls—I was all in! All of this in only the first five months.

Remember that guy I mentioned earlier, P.K. Knotts? Well, he approached me with an opportunity to discuss multicultural diversity that I could not believe. It was a meeting with the minister, Assistant Minister, Yuri Yamamoto, administrators of the congregation, and influential, lifelong members—and they wanted my input. I was blown away. All of a sudden, I didn't just have a Hip-Hop approach to my vocabulary—I had a voice. My voice mattered. Soon after, I became a Mosaic Maker, part of a nationwide group of activists in the fight to create a more culturally diverse UU experience. It was my way of seeing more open-minded people of color while encouraging an outreach to congregations of various religions and cultures for the sake of the future of Unitarian Universalism. It was right up my alley.

Before I knew it, I was at UUFR almost all the time. I loved it. But then, things started to take a strange turn.

Almost overnight, I began to feel two facets of my experience at UUFR: my involvement within the congregation and, adversely, a cultural polarization. It seemed like, all of a sudden, my wife and I had become the "token black couple." I'm sure it wasn't intentional, but it continued right under our noses. It seemed as though, no matter what lengths I would go to be recognized as just a person, I was placed in the category of "black." I began to realize that my newfound friend, P.K. Knotts, wanted us to embody that with the same vigor, to my dismay.

Lemme explain. The best possible way I can do so is in this fashion: Me being "black" is the same to me as being a "boy" or "girl" or a transgendered being. My wife and I do not place ourselves in that category. At all. And it's quite frustrating when anyone tries to put us in it. Our shared belief is simple: we are all...people of color. No black or white here. My *jacket* is black. These *words* are black. My way of life *isn't*. My skin color *isn't*. The way I *talk* isn't. The way I *walk* isn't. Still, people inherently categorize people as either black or white; they don't even think about it. That's separatism—point blank, <u>period</u>—and I *hate* being separated.

I'm sure you can imagine how my thoughts may have made people felt. Hell, I even blame myself for P.K. leaving because of that. To this day, I feel like I hurt him. In spite of that, I tried to create a movement within UUFR with that mindset.

Thoughts raged through me during the coming months as to how my message could be passed on to members of the congregation, in hopes that they would adopt this way of thinking. I had created a two-part Wellspring series entitled "The Hip-Hop Workshop," for which the classroom was packed both time. My intent was to enrich the minds of all present—to explain it as more than just an expression from a musician's standpoint, but as a worldwide culture of consciousness shared by all people who inhabit the earth.

I wanted everyone to leave the sessions with the truth—that Hip-Hop isn't "black music," but the sound of an entire culture that has spanned for a longer time than books or even than some people would care to allow. I wanted them leaving my workshop learning that we *all*... Hip-Hop.

This happened to little avail. Though both parts of the workshop were filled to the brim with participants, I felt as if I didn't reach everyone to the point of having them contemplate a new way of thinking toward the message I was trying to convey—the oneness of all things.

This past February, as a lay worship associate and UU Mosaic Maker dedicated to multicultural diversity, I took on the topic of the "Black Lives Matter" campaign in the latter end of a two-part homily alongside Rev. John Saxon in a way that most would have deemed abstract—by not claiming that phrase at all. Instead, I claimed my part of the sermon to be "All Lives Matter"—denouncing race altogether. In the end, I was still thought of as what one member described as "the representation of an angry, black man." This was not what I was going for—not at all.

I even vowed to create an "Unlearn" Wellspring series based on my beliefs that if we cease to study race and separatism, one generation at a time, the phenomenon will deplete into nothing. My basis for this argument came in the form of a fifty-five-second video clip from none other than Morgan Freeman, Academy Award–winning actor, who "solved racism in under sixty seconds." In the last seconds of the clip, Mr. Freeman states, "I'm going to stop calling you a white man, and in return, I ask that you stop calling me a black man."

Such a profound statement! I had thought. Knowingly, it was a pretty tall order, but I tried to get things rolling in that direction—also to no avail. I began to get exhausted. There was even a time that, after having so much of my efforts fall on what I presumed to be deaf ears,

I had contemplated my involvement with the church and almost quit attending.

But then it hit me. Hit me like a stray snowball in a sandstorm, as if the revelation had no earthly business even being there. It was the thought that "If I don't do this, who will?" And from that moment on, I realized my purpose at UUFR: to educate about our equality...by any...means... necessary. Not an equality of black and white, but an equality of color— all color—as human beings, just like any other human being. Through my time and talent, this is what I proclaim my purpose is at UUFR, and I will not waiver from it for anyone. And so, here I am.

I'm Mike Jenkins. Sole surviving male of my family name, husband to Sabrina Ayitevie-Jenkins, who's the mother of three preteen children. Personal trainer, fitness instructor, motivational speaker, and lay worship associate. Unitarian Universalist Mosaic Maker. Poet, Hip-Hop artist and scholar, better known by the alias "Tr1umphant." Owner of emerging company *Blaq Butterfly Wings*—dedicated to reaching a mountaintop the likes of Martin Luther King's last speech while encouraging the minds, bodies, and spirits of its patrons to grow stronger human beings.

I am Hip-Hop as a consciousness, as a culture, and as a product of that consciousness and culture—a trinity within myself. I am *not...a black person*. I am a person of color, just as *you* are. I am the human experience and the embodiment of all other decisions—be they one person's *yes* to another person's *no*—all at the same time. I am the microcosm of this macrocosmic omniverse, singing our life in lyrics without end—or beginning. And so are *you*. I'm now someone you can truly say you really, really know.

Whaddup.

Tr1umph@nt

UU Person of Color Personal Story

Christine Chao

I was a member of Throop Unitarian Universalist Church for about two years. I grew up in a predominantly secular home, although there were some Protestant Christian church visits when visiting my mother's side of the family. I discovered Unitarian Universalism as a young adult. I currently identify as an atheist/humanist.

My life has always flowed better when I am a part of a supportive spiritual community. I lost my mother at the age of nineteen and was supported by a Christian fellowship at school. Trying to make sense of life and coming to terms with this monumental loss, I was held by these loving, supportive classmates during that time. They made care packages for me and were able to pray with me to make sense of all the suffering and pain.

However, I really lost my mother at the age of nine due to mental illness. She suffered the last ten years of her life, and although it was for the best that she was no longer suffering, it did not make her physical passing any less painful.

Fast-forward a few years, and I was once again seeking another spiritual community, as I could not believe in the dogma of the more traditional Christian churches. I believed there are many ways to God/Universe/ what have you. All the great religions in the world have common truths. Love your neighbor as yourself. Do unto others as you would have them do unto you. Live your life well. I had never heard about Unitarian Universalism before finding this congregation through the Arroyo Time Bank and the Northeast Los Angeles (NELA) Transition community garden. I agreed with the seven UU principles, and I loved that it was a liberal, open-minded church that encouraged each person to find their own spiritual path.

Through the encouragement of my pastor, Tera Little, I was sponsored by the UUA to take part in the Unitarian Universalist Multicultural Leadership conference in Boston in September 2013. That conference was a powerful experience, as I was able to bear witness to the collective anger and pain of youths of African American descent who were questioning the recent Trayvon Martin shooting. We were instructed to always wear our name tag, as there had been an uncomfortable experience a few years back where a youth of color was confronted by a white UU as an intruder in the UUA headquarters.

I was inspired to take what I had learned in the conference and bring it back to our congregation. With the permission of Rev. Dr. Monica L. Cummings, I gave a workshop on gender identity and another one on race identity issues. There was little interest on the part of the congregants, with only three or four people showing up at each workshop. I am not sure if it was due to a lack of interest or a lack of publicity. It was in the weekly bulletin and announced during worship. What passion was generated soon fizzled out at my small home church, as life got busy for me as I made a career change and returned to school.

My father died unexpectedly of pulmonary fibrosis in April 2014 at the age of sixty-nine. I announced it on Facebook and received many condolences. I heard not a word from my home church. Four days later, I called and expressed my dismay that no one had reached out; maybe they had not seen the Facebook post? I requested help with boxing and moving my father's lifetime worth of belongings in two weeks' time. Some members heeded the call and came out to help. I was very grateful, but after that nothing, no reaching out.

I am not sure if this lack of care was because we do not have a critical mass in our congregation or because we are stuck in our intellectual talk about spirituality in UU churches. I knew this was an issue at our church as I was a part of the Pastoral Care Team, and there was so much need but not enough people or resources. Still, it was jarring to see the truth of the matter. You can choose your community, but does that mean they choose you as well?

While I appreciate that we can discuss things in depth, I believe UUs have good intentions but do not always put actions to those good intentions. If you do not have God to bind you together, what does bind you as a sacred community? It is all good to talk about being a connected, loving community, but where is this loving community when life becomes difficult through personal loss and when the shit hits the proverbial fan?

Personally, I also found my spiritual needs not always be met with hymns that did not touch me and messages that were nice to hear but often left me feeling a sense of lack. Nice church experiences, but no real depth. I made the difficult decision at the end of 2014 not to return to church. You can only give so much and love something so much, but when you are not getting the love and care in return, it is time to move on.

Eavesdropping—2

I try so hard, but it still does not feel right.
Something must be wrong with me.
I was sitting in this meeting with a bunch of white people
discussing how to bring more black people to our church.
I was objectified.
Why should black people care?

A Story of a Mexican Unitarian Universalist

Anonymous

I am originally from Mexico. Several years ago, I discovered Unitarian Universalism, and it was love at first sight. One day I took some friends to visit a large UU church, and while we were there, I was encouraged to apply for a part-time position to help a group of members who had been meeting at a public school's media center find a place to call their own, to coordinate worship at the new site, to plan events in the diverse neighborhood where we were located, and to engage with the Latino community.

This was about six months after I became a UU in 2009. I worked there for less than two years. There were two more people of color on staff, a Black receptionist and a Latino janitor. The receptionist left soon after I came onboard. She mentioned to me her ongoing struggles with several staff members. My work environment was less than welcoming from the very beginning, and it got gradually worse until it reached the point of being hostile, and I could no longer take it. It was greatly affecting my health.

Many of the behaviors of some staff members seemed to me to be highly hypocritical, considering the message UUs preach. My bilingualism was welcomed for the position I was filling, but some did not welcome my biculturalism and my ideas on how to accomplish the objectives that I was hired for.

As the coordinator of a church that had just settled into a new diverse community, I saw community outreach as an essential part of my job and represented my church in my many interactions with the community. This took a considerable amount of time, well beyond that of a part-time job. I was to do only what I was told to do, and everything else had to be done on my own time. I also got in trouble for not following proper protocol when situations arose in the community that required a rapid response. The line between being myself and being part of the staff became blurred.

When I decided to leave the job, I was told I had to stay away from the new campus for an entire year. So a rule meant for ministerial staff had been expanded and was being applied to me also. I objected to that, refused to sign the paper placed in front of me, and gave them my word only that I would stay away for six months to allow the new coordinator to connect with the congregation.

I was worried that all the works I had started at the church to connect with the community would fall apart if I did not return for a whole year. Indeed, the person who took over my responsibilities did not have time to continue all the work that I had started.

Eventually I did go back to the second campus to support it. I'm proud to have been part of its history and of the work we continue to do. Some of the people I had trouble working with are no longer part of the staff, but neither are some of the ones that came to my defense when they felt I was being unjustly treated. I still stay away from the main campus, except for special events, to avoid the painful memories.

The church has made a lot of progress since. The staff is slowly becoming more diverse. It's still challenging to get the main congregation to embrace issues that affect the community at large but not the majority of UUs, such as immigration and racism. In issues like these, the second campus leads the way.

Sometimes my faith community discourages me, but I am determined to stay and do what I can to help make it more welcoming not only to people of color but also to other groups that are greatly underrepresented in the pews, such as active-duty military members and veterans.

Chandra Snell's Journey to Unitarian Universalism—and Back

Chandra Snell

Funny how I had always taken for granted that there were "White" Churches of Christ—the denomination I grew up in—and "Black" ones. Occasionally, a White Church of Christ preacher from a nearby congregation would preach. During his (and it was always *his*) sermon, the men in the "amen corner" would shout encouraging, "Preach it!" "Well!" "Come on with it!" etc., after which the White preacher would invariably say something to the effect of "Gee, *my* congregation never reacts with such enthusiasm."

Sometimes White people would visit. They usually looked bewildered or otherwise unbalanced somehow. Congregants seemed to go out of their way to make them feel more at home, but they almost never came back. If they were daring enough to get baptized and become members, some member or other would usually "helpfully" let them know that such-and-such congregation (that is, a White congregation) wasn't very far away, and that they might like it. And usually, newly baptized White members did, or at least they never came back.

After you reach a certain age in the South (and, contrary to popular notions, South Florida, despite its multiculturalism and big-city ways, is still the South), you take the notion of "race" for granted. For us post-Civil Rights Era African American kids, however, this was not necessarily a negative. We would notice whether a person appeared Asian, Hispanic, White or Black, just as you would notice whether that person was fat or skinny, short or tall; there did not have to be a value judgment attached. Race just *was*.

For me, the negative associations did not creep in until I was in high school. At that point—during my racial "awakening"—White people devolved from mere curiosities occasionally floating somewhere around the perimeter of my consciousness to full-blown aliens.

My journey to Unitarian Universalism appears to be a confluence of certain strands of my life coming together: the sociocultural, the spiritual, and the personal.

I grew up in a fundamentalist, literalist religious tradition—Church of Christ—that denied (based on its biblical interpretation) the voices and gifts of women. My paternal grandparents were among the founders of a congregation in Fort Lauderdale, Florida, which later became very prominent in the community. (In fact, my grandparents partially raised the man who would later become—and still is—the minister.) My father and loads of extended relatives grew up in this congregation, and I'm told I made my debut there at two weeks old. My mother was baptized (coming from the Baptist tradition) into this church when I was a young child.

Everyone in the congregation knew who I was, and church was literally my extended family, since my relatives comprised a good bit of the membership. After hearing a terrifying sermon regarding "weeping and gnashing of teeth," during which I envisioned disembodied dentures snapping at me, I was baptized into this church at the age of nine. It was no question that all who were not in our church were going to hell.

Throughout my childhood and well into adulthood, I was relieved and grateful that I had been born into "the truth," and therefore did not need to reject a previously held belief system in order to be "saved." It eluded me how others apparently were intentionally blind to "the truth." I felt sorry for them.

I enjoyed "playing church" as a child (with me always cast as the preacher) and reveled in the many activities that were available to youth. Like many African American children, I honed my public speaking skills during special presentations for Easter, Black History Month, and Thanksgiving programs. I also assisted my mother in teaching a children's Bible class, sang with the youth group, and served on the Meals on Wheels committee. I loved all these activities.

But, once I grew up, these opportunities to serve within the church were severely curtailed. The only options available to women were as Sunday school or Bible study teachers in women's classes, and there were only so many of those positions to go around, of course! Looking back, this is when my long slide into "bench warming" began. Once I stopped being meaningfully (for me) involved in the life of the church, it became dry duty and obligation.

Oddly, I now realize, the Church of Christ supported women's equality in nearly every arena save the religious; educationally, professionally, and socially, girls and women were implicitly encouraged to achieve at the highest levels, and our congregation's women overwhelmingly worked outside the home. However, we still believed and accepted a strict interpretation of Paul's words concerning women's roles within the church.

As with many youth, my church attendance and involvement slacked off considerably during my college years. After graduation and moving away from my hometown, I met my husband-to-be at another Church of Christ congregation. Once I had a child, I resolved to buckle down and get serious again about church (with decidedly mixed results). I tried to take advantage of the service opportunities that came my way (few and far between) and even envisioned—during a kind of spiritual growth spurt, I suppose—at one point becoming a full-time speaker at women's church events.

After leaving the congregation in which I'd met my husband and had my child to follow my husband to yet another Church of Christ congregation, I became increasingly disaffected. It may have been partially due to the cultural disconnect (this new one was a White congregation), my as-yet unrecognized spiritual discontent, or a combination of both. Yet I limped on, mainly because I didn't perceive that I had a choice. After all, I didn't want to damn my soul for all eternity.

One conversation with a coworker during this time stuck with me. I forget what we were talking about, but I brought up "God" at some point in the discussion. My coworker (a very intelligent guy whose opinion I respected) said incredulously, "You believe in God?!" Affronted, I responded in the affirmative. He said, "Haven't you read Joseph Campbell? *The Power of Myth*?" Needless to say, I had not. I left the conversation feeling sorry for my coworker, a kind, affable soul who I assumed wouldn't be walking through the pearly gates.

I don't recall the specific impetus that led me to begin researching the history of the Church of Christ, but one thing that I remember striking me was the fact that it's an overwhelmingly Southern institution. *Why is that*, I wondered, *if we have "the truth"? Why are most Churches of Christ confined to the South?*

I read about how the Disciples of Christ and Churches of Christ both have common Presbyterian (that is, Protestant) origins. We were not unique! I also, for the first time, read about the history and impact of racial segregation in the church (which remains, de facto, to this day). Funny how I had always taken for granted the fact that there were White congregations and Black ones. I had never questioned why this was so; I had always just accepted it as a fact of life.

And finally, came the kicker, which was a sucker punch to my gut: the Church of Christ, in its current manifestation, came into existence only a little more than a hundred years ago—not during the Day of Pentecost, as I had been told all my life! If my church was mistaken about this, then what else was it wrong about?

For a while, I felt adrift, as I had nothing with which to replace my former belief system. I also experienced an undercurrent of anxiety, feeling pressure to find what was really "the truth," because there could obviously be only one "true" church, right? I didn't tell anyone in my family about my confusion, certain that they would condemn me for even having questions; I certainly condemned myself for having doubts.

After much thought, prayer, and reflection, I left the Church of Christ to join a Black United Methodist Church, whose biblical interpretation embraced a plethora of roles for women within the church, honoring and affirming their spiritual gifts—not confining them to second-class citizenship. I had come to the conclusion that no single church held a monopoly on truth, since, as far as I could determine, they were all imperfect, man-made institutions, however well meaning. I decided that the only "true" church was the one in which a particular individual could best grow spiritually; this was the only criterion that came to make any sense to me.

I blossomed in the UMC, both spiritually and personally, sharing my gifts and talents with a fullness of heart that I never imagined possible. My religion evolved from one of mere obligation to one of joy.

I thought my spiritual seeking was over and that I would rest in this new spiritual home forever. However, that was not to be the case (much to my chagrin—at least initially). I found that I still had questions and that they would not go away. Worse yet, I found that old boogeyman of dry duty and obligation hounding me once again.

Thus, for about a year of once again seeking, praying, reading (especially Joseph Campbell—finally!—and Karen Armstrong), and reflecting, I decided to join the Unitarian Universalist Church. Though I still didn't have the answers (and likely never will), this church was the perfect fit for me at that point in my journey because it encouraged questions and seeking, and it fully engaged my mind.

But I still retained membership in the UMC, for many reasons. Contrary to the biblical admonition that one cannot serve two masters, I found that my UU and UMC memberships complemented one another, more often than not. While I was more comfortable culturally in the UMC, Unitarian Universalism was a better fit, spiritually and intellectually. While maintaining a (semi) active presence in both was sometimes tiring, I needed both because, together, that joint membership worked for me.

Since I first began writing this essay in 2014, I started the ordination process to become a deacon in the UMC. Instead of finding a contradiction between the two denominations, I've found that my Unitarian Universalism was inclusive of, and allowed me to more fully embrace, the UMC—perhaps in ways that would not have been possible for me without Unitarian Universalism.

I believed that my spirit was leading me to serve my community as an ordained deacon in the UMC, without diminishing my Unitarian Universalism. Although it was puzzling to some, being active within both the UUC and the UMC was part of my faith journey and enhanced my perspective regarding religion, faith, and spirituality.

However, in mid-September of 2015, I officially resigned from my membership at the UU Church in order to devote myself fully to the ordination process. Nevertheless, Unitarian Universalism has been an important part of my faith journey.

Eavesdropping—3

You can't generalize that all people of color have
bad experiences in a UU congregation.
I love my church.
My church is very diverse!

Eavesdropping—4

I am a Universalist, so I am not interested
in a people-of-color meeting.
No, I did not realize that some people of color
had a hard time in a UU church.

Experiences of a Puerto Rican Unitarian Universalist

Anonymous

I grew up Catholic, am forty years old, and have been a Unitarian Universalist since 2009. I found it after taking belief.net online quiz, which told me I was 99 percent UU, even though I didn't know what that was. I then Googled it.

Our UU congregation is on a prime piece of real estate, surrounded by gated upper-middle-class homes worth a minimum of $350,000. It makes me wonder if our congregation's lack of diversity has something to do with our location.

There are fewer than ten Latinos in my two-hundred-plus UU congregation. I simply do not fit in at a 98 percent affluent, white congregation, where coffee hour and dinner parties consist of discussing your last trip to Europe. We do have an increasing Latin community around here that fled Venezuela, Colombia, Brazil, Peru, Argentina, and other countries. I have seen some of them visiting, but they don't tend to stay.

It's the little things that keep minorities and lower-income people away from my particular UU, such as the lack of diverse music. My church plays folk and classical mostly, though during summer services, some speakers play a handful of popular songs.

Then there are the uptight Christmas Eve services. And the elitism: people bragging about their trips to Europe and their graduate degrees, looking down on blue-collar workers. The services focus on UU history and involve highly philosophical sermons that an average Joe will not get. Then there is a lack of Spanish sermons in cities with large Hispanic populations.

I am an agnostic and personally prefer nontraditional services with joyful music, drumming, less history and philosophy, and more relatable sermons. I enjoy the sermons available online from All Souls in Tulsa, Oklahoma. They got it right, in my opinion.

I visit the local UU congregation occasionally when I know of a good speaker coming, but I simply don't belong there. I don't think a multicultural initiative or group would be welcomed there either, and there are not enough people of color to support it. I admit I did not try to form one, out of fear of rejection and lack of time.

I am going to the Christian Spanish church this weekend, where I do fit in racially and economically as a struggling working mother—even though I am agnostic and will secretly question what the preacher says. Sad. A Puerto Rican working-class agnostic needs more choices! My time is limited with a toddler at home and while working full time. I cannot join the conference calls [of UUs of color] but will enjoy continuing to read the emails, knowing I am not alone. I wish in twenty years people like me feel welcomed at UU congregations.

My UU Story

Lily Boyce

I am Lakota, light skinned, urban, and have been in foster care, a teenage runaway, and in recovery from drugs and alcohol abuse for more than twenty-five years. I have been trying to finish my bachelor's degree for years and keep dropping out due to depression and other things. I work in helping fields and just keep struggling on. I am also raising two grandchildren, ages seventeen and four.

I've worked as a family advocate in mental health and child welfare. I am looking for a different way to help the same folks—folks like me. I find social work to be missing the spirit part of helping people. Racism, classism, and patriarchy are also embedded in social work systems and theories. The voices that seem to express solutions best are women who have studied social justice theology. So I am thinking of trying to go to Iliff School of Theology to work on a degree that combines social work and theology.

I used to attend Jefferson Unitarian Church in Golden. In many ways, it was a welcoming, wonderful church. I really liked the main preacher, Peter Morales, who now is the head of the Unitarian Universalist Association. Though I liked him, he was getting ready to move on. I participated in some groups that were wonderful. They even discussed issues of people of color. We also did work with American Indian tribes and helped the homeless community—all reasons I liked them.

I found the people very kind and earnest. I really haven't found any other spiritual community that is a better fit for me. But, still, almost everyone was white and well-heeled.

One challenge I had was with the church choir and my granddaughter. They met at four in the afternoon on a weekday. It seemed all the other kids' families had a stay-at-home parent, so rehearsal during work hours wasn't a problem for them. After my granddaughter missed rehearsals, she was asked to leave the choir. The fact that she couldn't read well and thus had trouble reading the music didn't go over well either.

Another challenge for me was, in one sermon, it was pronounced proudly that Unitarian children tend toward the upper end of the IQ spectrum or educational attainment, compared to other religions. And the minister spent some time fleshing that out. Well, my granddaughter was in an enclosed behavioral classroom with severe ADHD. She was barely literate.

Finding a good spiritual community for her was more of a priority than finding one for me. My granddaughter, although Lakota through my blood, has light skin, blue eyes, and appears to be white. Because in the Indian community white folks trying to "go native" is not looked on too favorably, I was unhappy with the way my granddaughter was treated by some. I wanted to give her and my daughters—who also were raised in traditionalism but do not seem inclined to follow it—a spiritual community they could turn to if they ever choose to search. (I can always go to ceremonies if I need to.) So the intellectual elitism I heard in that sermon hit a sour note for me and added to my feeling of not fitting in.

There were other little things. Each alone would have been nothing to sweat, but taken together, all led me to feel like I did not see this as a spiritual home for my family. For example, there was the heavy emphasis on financial giving. While that was necessary for the church to go on and thrive, I was struggling to make ends meet. I felt guilt-ridden if

I couldn't make my monthly contribution. The guilt was part of my decision to no longer attend.

Another little thing: when I just sat and visited, I found in conversations with other parishioners that their reality was very different from mine. Politically we were in general agreement, which is head and shoulders above most other religious communities these days. But in day-to-day life, we were way different. So I drifted away, but I haven't found a spiritual community that I like or resonate with more than Unitarian Universalism.

So here I am, with a four-year-old grandson I am raising who looks to be part black and other. Again, when I think of going to Jefferson Unitarian Church, I remember there wasn't a lot of color there. As I think of a community for my grandkids, I try to visualize UU but have trouble seeing it.

When I am in a good space, I do better in that type of community. I just found the upper-middle-class white culture hard to take when I wasn't doing well. I had a feeling that if I brought struggling friends from my community, they wouldn't feel comfortable there. These feelings contributed to my decision not to attend anymore.

I keep thinking of going to the one downtown but haven't made it there yet. Parking is a problem.

Letting Go of Faith to Be Whole Again

Elías Ortega-Aponte

In seminary, I made the decision to let go of my faith. I realized that my understanding of faith at that time no longer sustained me. The irony was not lost on me, but I considered letting go my faith a necessary step towards a more authentic me, and in seminary from all places. It was ironic because there I was, in the place where many go to peruse deeper into what they believe, to figure out layers of meanings to faith practices, and to reflect seriously on the teachings and practices of religious traditions in search of ministerial capacitation, consciously moving away from all of it. And it was there, in seminary, where I finally decided to let go of the Christian faith that had so far sustained me. Letting go of faith was an act of self-protection. I recognized that the journey to fulfill my vocation as a theological educator required the risk of losing my understanding of faith. In fact, seeking spiritual maturity and authenticity might indeed need such a risk. While at the time I was not sure what that would entail, I sensed that it had something to do with making an intentional choice of not accepting the status quo and comfort of a preshaped understanding of faith; a faith inherited which I had not, with intention, made my own.

At least initially, since I was not attending seminary to pursue a ministry call, the thought of leaving Christianity behind did not bother me much. My intent was clear: I needed to take a deeper and more serious look at faith, and I felt like I needed to chart a different path moving forward.

My attitude toward a seminary education was more about exploring what religion meant to me, more about intellectual curiosity than a need to be steeped in a particular tradition. My approach was to enter seminary with a mind as open as I could muster. I felt secured that, while everything I had held truth to my faith life was negotiable, I would be okay at the end. Later, I recognized that in my particular path, lessons, ideas, and long-ago learned conceptions would follow me. As I shifted toward seeing the world through humanist lenses, the Christian teachings that shaped my faith growing up colored these lenses. So, I became a religious humanist with Christian sensibilities.

The experiences in seminary that led me down this road were more personal than intellectual. It was not about being argued out of a position, but rather having to fight through a social and political landscape that made me reconsider Christianity. I did not leave Christianity solely as a matter of intellectual reflection or spiritual conviction. Rather, I needed to leave my spiritual home as an act of self-protection, as a way to get distance from the whiteness and colonizing power of Christianity in a mainline Protestant seminary and what that meant for my well-being.

It was in a Protestant seminary, exploring faith among others who had a similar desire, that I experienced a level of racism and sexism like I had not experienced before. As an Afro-Latino, I have flesh knowledge of how racism and sexism operate. My stories are one more link in the chain of the collective memories of boys and girls, elders and ancestors of color. The difference at a seminary for me was that religion was not a safe place; the very structure of it justified the watchdogs of white supremacy. Up to that point in my life, religion had provided a safe and nurturing place, but now I was also aware of the colonizing power of the thoughts, symbols, and spaces of Christian religiosity.

I felt that colonizing gaze whenever I stepped into a space demarcated by such symbols—even my living space. I could not find solace in Christianity. It is true that I had good mentors and friends while in seminary; I entered into lifelong friendships with some of them that have enriched my life and that of my family. But I also had experiences that made me wonder whether I wanted to remain in close contact with most of those belonging to such circles. I became bitter and increasingly angry at the virulent racism that followed me around campus. I was increasingly frustrated by the ways in which daily experiences of microaggression permeated my life and was upset with how these experiences made me question past happenings, how they forced a reframing of the past.

In self-protection, I left the church. It was a move away from a religion demarcated more by an institutional identity than by life-giving and preserving spiritual practices as it was a struggle with notions of the divine. However, over time, it has been difficult for me to differentiate between the institutions and the beliefs they enshrine.

Take Christianity and monotheism for example. Somewhere in me, there were moments when I felt a need to call out to something larger than myself. I'm not sure what. But one thing was clear: I would continue struggling with the thought of "once Pentecostal, always Pentecostal." I'd heard this saying many times growing up. How would this play out for me, a Pentecostal outside of Christianity? A humanist who was also a Pentecostal—at least sometimes? Would that even be possible?

During this time of deep anger and my exodus from Christianity, my partner and I welcomed our first child into our lives. What a divine blessing! We had both grown deeply religious, but through different paths, and we had both become disenchanted with Christianity. Nevertheless, we shared a longing to find a spiritual home. But where? We knew that, at least at the moment, we would not be going to a Christian congregation, nor were we particularly comfortable with visiting a house of worship where we would be required to hold to theistic beliefs. Where would we be going?

***

While biking along the streets of Princeton, New Jersey, I recalled seeing a UU congregation. Having no idea what Unitarian Universalism meant, I decided to do a quick check online. I liked what I read about UUs. I spent some time reading up on the Seven Principles, and after some reflection, I decided to give it a try. What I read sounded familiar enough to what I was used to and yet distinct enough to make it seem a fresh possibility. I did not tell my partner about it since I was not sure how she would react to my exploration of a new spiritual community. I just went and checked it out under the pretense of going for an extended bike ride.

The worship experience felt different. I felt a moment of perhaps this may be a good place to be. I put the bug in my partner's ear, insisting that we check it out. After all, both of us had grown up in churches and spending Sunday mornings in a place of worship was normal to us, so why not?

Shortly after my first visit, we picked a Sunday to attend together. In our next visit, the then minister of the congregation, Rev. Ian Forrest Gilmore, preached a sermon titled "Bible Self-Defense." It was a cathartic moment for both of us. We felt that day that we had found a place to call a spiritual home.

A decade into my journey as a UU, I still feel that I have found a spiritual home. My experiences as a UU have allowed me to experience a degree of healing, centering, and recommitment to a religious life that I thought doubtful during and after my seminary experience. Furthermore, I can find a place to wrestle with the questions of faith that led me to seminary in the first place. Some answers I have found; others I am still searching for.

Some of these things resonate with why many remain committed to being UU, such as the strong moral compass of our religious tradition that affirms the dignity of humans and the natural work alike. A commitment to works for justice for all, even if we often fall short of this goal. The embrace of the challenge to be a spiritual seeker and be open to new ways of understanding, seeing, and being in the world.

But not everything is good. Some experiences have been painful and somewhat disconcerting for me. These experiences are centered on being a person of color in a mostly white religious denomination.

At the time I found UU, I was willing to negotiate the ways in which I would interact or not "in a racial sense." I would pick and choose if and when to engage in racial conversations. While this may sound odd to some, it is a common experience for people of color in the United States; code switching is a necessary survival skill. After all, my partner and I were not sure how deeply we were going to commit; we approached the whole affair as being present, contributing in small ways to community life. And not being engaged was about right to me for a time. A deeper engagement on my part would have meant facing the ways in which my newfound spiritual home resembled the things I was moving out of when I left Christianity.

Even though I've found a home among UUs, talking about what it has been like for me as a UU of color to participate and worship in sacred spaces where I am not fully seen has been difficult. I have been unsure how much to push what I see as a need for deeper sacred conversations around racial justice.

But as time goes by, it is more difficult for me to remain silent. How do I respond when I hear of past actions of white UUs in the racial struggles in the United States in terms that make their contributions not only equal to but sometimes central to the work done by communities of color? How do I respond to the practice of finding out which civil rights heroes had UU connections, like Gandhi and Martin Luther King Jr., and others, finding ways in which UU ideas shaped them? More importantly, how do I raise questions around our ongoing commitment to real transformative racial justice work that does not rest on the past but looks toward future possibilities? I don't mean for my questions to cast doubt on the work UUs have done around racial justice, but rather to call attention to the ways in which our communal stories are told may appropriate—and at worst colonize—the struggles of those not fully represented in our midst.

Racial erasure is but one of the ways in which I have felt invisible among UUs. Another way has been religious erasure. Can I be simultaneously UU and Pentecostal? How would people react if I shared with them that I felt moved by the Spirit to pray for them? What would be people's reaction if I were to shout in the middle of the service when touched by something meaningful, by a word that spoke to me directly? Just as the ways in which we talk about race often erase racial struggles of folks in our midst, I fear that our collective ways of presenting ourselves religiously are not as welcoming as we claim.

I am not sure what the future will entail for me as a UU, but when I think of that future, I sense that it will mean that I will be a Pentecostal UU of color, fully committed to justice-making work and unapologetic about my body and my faith.

An Interview with P.K. Knotts

Yuri Yamamoto: Thank you for agreeing to share your stories. Tell me a little bit about yourself.

P.K.: I'm not just one person all the time. I have multiple personalities, lots of interest. One consistent thing is that I'm deeply spiritual and see the world being united and doing my part to make it happen. I'm a Unitarian. I always have been, even before I heard of the Unitarian Universalist denomination. When I say *Unitarian*, I'm talking about seeing the world as different cultures, different ideas, different religions, but yet being one human family and understanding that I'm a part of all of it. Now, I may have been born African American, but there is a part of me that embraces Asian cultures. There is a part of me that embraces European cultures. I am not just one thing. Because of that, I recognize that we are all important contributors to each other. That's what I mean by Unitarian. I am all of these things.

Yuri: When did you come to know about Unitarian Universalism?

P.K.: I heard about Unitarian Universalism when I was a sophomore in college. I was assigned to read Emerson's "Divinity School Address." And from there I discovered many other writers who had a Unitarian Universalist bent. But I did not embrace them. It was maybe thirty years ago that a friend of mine invited me to come to her church, Unitarian Universalist Fellowship of Raleigh (UUFR), one Sunday morning. I was intrigued by it, although that was the only time I attended. Then, twenty-years later, I decided to visit UUFR. It was a lot bigger church with more members and also a lot different than what I had remembered.

Yuri: What was it like to visit that church?

P.K.: When I visited it thirty years ago, it was in a smaller building, and there were not as many members. I probably met two thirds of the congregation, which left me with a very good feeling about coming back twenty-five years later. In contrast to my first visit, there was a stark difference. It appeared to me as if the warmth of the congregation that I so fondly remembered was no longer in this new congregation in this new building. That had dramatically changed. If I were perfectly honest, I would probably say that I was taken aback by the new experience.

It was obviously not the same kind of welcoming experience. I was greeted at the door, given the morning's program, and that was it—and asked to stand up if new visitors. But as far as anything else, I was just kind of lost in the crowd. I went downstairs for coffee hour afterward. I had coffee and kind of milled around. Because I was expecting something different, I had no idea that I was gonna have to work so hard just to get to know people, and it's not my personality to be overtly gregarious in some new situations. So I just had coffee and moved around and said hello to people, but there were no real connections, no real conversations.

Yuri: Why did you come back then?

P.K.: The first sermon that I heard by the then-minister, Tom Rhodes, was a message that I needed to hear. The tone of the message was the idea of all things being one, which was what I was looking for, the sense of unity. I came back the next week because I wanted to hear more of where he was going. He was teaching again next Sunday, and I thoroughly enjoyed it. But this Sunday I was expecting that having been there the previous Sunday, and the people had seen me there, I would be approached during coffee hour. But that did not happen, which left me with a bit of dichotomy: I was enjoying hearing the lead minister, but I wasn't having any interactions with the congregants, which is necessary for me. I need to connect with the people around me, not just the person at the top.

Yuri: Did you try to talk with the minister?

P.K.: I met him at the door as I exited to go downstairs and had as much of a conversation that could be held in a minute or two. There was a sense of warmth, genuineness, as well as intellectual stimulation that I received from him there. It was encouraging. I liked him, to say the least.

Yuri: Were you able to establish any connections with the congregation eventually?

P.K.: Yes. At some point, I'd made the decision that I was gonna give it one more try, and if I didn't connect with the congregation then, I would not come back. During the week, at a job site, one of the ladies was making a conversation about my hat. So on that Sunday morning, I grabbed a hat and went to the service and enjoyed it once again. There was something about the third service with the music that kind of resonated with me. So I felt pretty good when I went downstairs for coffee hour. As I was finishing coffee, one of the congregants walked up to me and kind of tapped me on the back of my hat and said, "Hey, I like that hat." And I turned and I saw this bright, smiling face, a face I hadn't seen before, welcoming and inviting. And I responded, "Yeah, this is one of my favorites. No, you can't have it." From there we sparked up the conversation, and I ended up talking with her the rest of coffee hour and went to lunch immediately after. I was genuinely taken by this person, and she was what I was hoping for in a congregation. So that was encouraging enough for me to come back next week, and I continued to return on alternating Sundays from that point.

I wanted to make a decision whether I wanted to stay here at UUFR or go to a Unity church. At that time, I was looking for a new congregation, but I really wanted to connect with each one of them before I made a decision as to whether or not I was going to be a part of one. Unity churches are generally smaller. They are more welcoming. They also have a spiritual message that resonates with me. It leans more toward Christianity than sometimes I'm comfortable with. At UUFR, there was very little mention of God and the teachings of Christ. Because I think that all the world religions have something to offer, when we limit ourselves to just Christianity, we are doing ourselves a disservice. Even though Unity church does embrace world religions, there is more of a leaning toward the metaphysical aspect of Christianity.

I was brought up a dyed-in-the-wool Southern Baptist. My grandparents were church seed sowers. They would go into small communities and build up churches. They put together the physical buildings, then attracted congregants and a pastor for them. So I had lots of experiences in the African American version of the Southern Baptist Church. I don't know when I was old enough to say to my grandmother that I wanted to do something different other than going to church with her. I began to explore the Nation of Islam and embraced the idea of economic security through developing your own businesses. But that, too, was not big enough for me. I always had a sense that if there is a god, he or she is a lot bigger than any of us can ever understand or explain or even begin to write rules for and about it. So I've always been uncomfortable with God being explained as one thing as opposed to something else. I've probably been a seeker for most of my life.

Yuri: What happened after you got connected with one person at UUFR?

P.K.: Well, the next Sunday, this person, Tracy, met me at the door. And I sat with her and she introduced me to the people around her. From there I just decided, *Hey, I can do this. It's worth it.* I, too, began, then, to take initiative in coming in early and greeting people. I had been so disappointed with the experience of not having met anyone that I had arranged to have a lunch with Tom Rhodes. I spelled out to him that I almost decided against UUFR if it had not been for Tracy approaching me. And I said to him that this is not the experience that I had some twenty-five years earlier and that I found it hard to believe that this was a current way the visitors were treated.

He and I talked about some of my ideas about how to change that. I gave him lots of ideas. And I was contacted by the assistant minister about implementing some of those ideas and if I would be willing to recruit greeters. I was kind of taken aback because he was presenting to me the same ideas that I'd presented to Tom, as if they were his ideas. So I pulled back and said I would recruit but wouldn't head it. Don't give me my ideas as if they are your own and expect that I'm going to accept it.

Yuri: How is the church in terms of diversity of people?

P.K.: I think at any given Sunday you would be hard-pressed to find, say, five African Americans, five Hispanics, five Asians, five people who are just poor, five people who don't have a college education among two hundred or so people attending the service. It's not very diverse. It's pretty much a white middle-class fellowship. I don't have any problems with those. The problem that I have is with the opening statement that we are a diverse and welcoming congregation. If you are telling me that I am invited and that I am appreciated and that I'm wanted on the one hand but then that is not my experience, I have a serious problem with that.

Yuri: Did you continue to feel unwelcome?

P.K.: No. After I began to know people, everyone wanted me to do this, to be on this committee, on that committee, be a part of this social function or another social function. But everywhere I went to, I would find that I was generally the only one black there. So I felt like I was a token face. I am also uncomfortable with that. I don't want to be the token black.

Yuri: Are you still a member of that congregation?

P.K.: I haven't attended service there for a while, but still am a member. I still have not decided whether or not I will return on a full-time basis. There are a lot of questions. There is some movement to change the experience that I had so that many other future visitors will not experience that. But it's a very slow movement, and it's not led very well. So I'm reluctant because I don't want to rock the boat. Because I operate on a much faster timetable, I have a lot less tolerance for having to convince people that it's in their interest to do the thing that they're saying that they are already doing.

Yuri: Were you attending every Sunday for a while?

P.K.: Yes.

Yuri: What happened?

P.K.: Well, after a couple of years, I had a young daughter who committed suicide. And I had kept the congregation aware that she had attempted suicide a couple of times, and I was always running back and forth to Maryland on a regular basis, just trying to help her to get stabilized. I reported on a Sunday morning in Joys and Sorrows that she had successfully committed suicide. And as I walked back to my seat, a couple of people kind of reached out and touched me on the arm, and others gave me their obligatory, "I am so sorry." I didn't feel like staying around after the service, and my friend Tracy wasn't there that Sunday. So I went home.

All week long I couldn't work. I was at home. My phone didn't ring once. I didn't get a card or anything. I didn't attend the following Sunday. When I did come back, it was like nothing had happened. And when I walked through the door, I was just another person coming in. But I was in pain. I can't tell you exactly what I was looking for, but I was looking for some kind of comfort, some kind of support from this congregation, people that I sat at men's meetings with. I'd been to circle dinners; I'd been on committees.

Nothing. It was like an empty void. It was like something kicked me in the stomach. And so I went home, and I thought about it. But there was nothing there.

Now, it is fair to say that I did get calls and offers of support from the staff. I appreciated their calls and willingness to help, but I felt like they were only doing their job, what they were paid to do. It wasn't like this was coming from people I sat out in the pews with on a regular basis, who I rubbed shoulders with, shared laughs and stories and other experiences with. And that part left me empty.

I attended a couple more times infrequently, but that feeling that I had developed just began to grow, and I felt like I had to get away from it. So I left. I was gone for a little over a year. And then I once again returned. That's probably attributed more to a couple of the staff, who were persistent in their efforts. That was when I decided that if I really wanted to see some things differently, then I would have to do that myself. I started talking to people about the idea of increasing the numbers of the ethnic communities and the poor so that they had a voice, they could effect some changes within the congregation.

It started off very well. I started off by bringing the idea to one of the committees that I was in, Journey Toward Wholeness. And it was rapidly embraced. We decided to put that into our mission statement. And from there I partnered up with one of the white members, and she made a presentation to the board that we would actually make that a part of mission statement of the church. When that was adopted, she and I began working together to build a team to investigate how we could make diversity more meaningful within that congregation. And along with the team members and music director, we put together our first meaningful diversity service. And from there we followed it up with a brainstorm session that had roughly twenty-five to thirty people. Together we presented our proposal to the board, which was adopted by the board and the membership. I thought we were well on our way to putting together a real meaningful program toward reaching the level of diversity I would have been comfortable with.

Yuri: Which is?

P.K.: I just think that a congregation is better served when they are not so homogeneous. When there are blacks and whites and Hispanics and Asians. When there are poor people, undereducated people, single mothers who are rearing families, and fathers who are unemployed. When they are all part of one community, I think we are stronger and we will work together to meet the needs of each other. We'd learn from each other. We'd support each other. That's what I believe. That's what I consider Unitarian. And even if the congregation was still sixty-five/thirty-five, I would be comfortable with that because there would be enough people who are not of the majority so that they collectively have a voice. So that's what I would hope to see in any congregation, regardless of what the numbers are. There are enough people to have a meaningful voice, have a meaningful effect, on the whole.

Yuri: Do you feel that your movement was embraced by people of color as well as white people in your congregation?

P.K.: I think it was. After four or five years of being around there and accosting people in the hallways, in the men's room, at coffee hour, when they came in the door, I always had the same message. The people began listening to what I was saying. Also, my beautiful white partner, Lynda, has this very quiet way of dealing with people, whereas I'm kind of rambunctious. She was able to reach people because she was genuinely interested, and she has been there for thirty-plus years. If she is looking for a change, more people are willing to listen to her. I was very effective with young people, people of color, other people who are underrepresented, and just that progressive part of our congregation that always had a revolutionary fervor. But even within the progressive UUFR, there is a conservative wing. And it's with those people that I found the most resistance. Silent but still there.

Yuri: Can you tell me a little bit more about the resistance?

P.K.: There were some people who were against diversity. Their arguments went something like "it's not that we oppose diversity, but I think that we don't have the kind of music that African Americans like or we don't have bilingual speakers. If we brought in too many poor people then we have budget problems." One argument in a meeting about changing the bylaws was that all members needed to commit to the generosity campaign, and if some people couldn't afford it, then they should get some exemption. This argument to me is a smokescreen that says that if you can't afford it, you shouldn't be here. And I took an exception to that. If you are going to open the door, if you're gonna say that you are welcoming, there shouldn't be in small print "but you got to have to be able to finance the program."

Yuri: Is that the reason you are not attending there anymore?

P.K.: That's probably 65 percent of the reason I'm not there. I just got tired of having to convince people that it's in their best interest to do the thing that they say they are doing, because when people walk in the door they can see it. You don't have to look very far to see it's not very welcoming. It's not very diverse, you know. Regardless how many times you repeat it, it doesn't make it true.

Yuri: What is your prognosis for the congregation?

P.K.: I think that without a dynamic, strong leadership in this area twenty-five years from today, they'd still be putting force the idea that they are warm, welcoming, diverse community, and the face of the congregation will look pretty much the same as it is today.

Yuri: Did you feel you were not effective in that congregation?

P.K.: No, I think I was very effective—just began to move the congregation toward formally adapting meaningful diversity as a part of its mission statement. It'd been presented to the congregation as our goal. I was very successful in recruiting a lot of people to become a part of the movement, very successfully convincing people that saying something just does not make it happen. I think I was very effective in presenting ideas about how to achieve it.

They don't have a strong leader currently. There are an awful lot of good-hearted people at UUFR. I really call many of them my friends. It's a beautiful place. And I think that once enough people begin to take the idea seriously of having meaningful diversity at that congregation, UUFR can be a shining place upon a hill because it has everything that it needs to grow. It has hard-working, smart, generous, committed individuals. It has the financial resources. It has the people resources. And it has the intellectual capacity for expanding, reaching, and growing. But they have yet to pull it all together. People kind of congregate together, like people from like incomes or like neighborhoods. And even though there are outreaches, they don't expand far enough. They don't go out into the community to get to know the community. They are expecting the community to come to them. It's not happening.

Yuri: What would make you want to go back?

P.K.: Well, a lot of the problems with any congregation is the history that we bring with us as individual members. And I understand that part of my history is that I don't have a lot of patience or a lot of tolerance for what I call *nonsense*. "Let's study this. We will vote on this at our next meeting, which is a year off." You know, putting things off into the future. I also want to have more direct, hands-on involvement from the staff, especially the minister, the associate minister, the social justice coordinator, taking a leading role in reformulating the makeup of the congregation—taking a leading role, not sitting back and waiting for the members to do the work while they take credit. Don't expect other people to do all of the work.

One night I saw the lead minister when I came there to recruit people to come to the forum on meaningful diversity. And the minister's response to me was "You know, meaningful diversity, that's dirty work." And I said to myself, *What? You? This is your congregation. I thought, as being the lead minister, you would be interested in the health of your congregation.* And to make a statement like that really rubbed me the wrong way. I know it's dirty work because some people are gonna be pissed off because you are upsetting the apple cart. But at least I have balls to say, "Look, it hasn't worked like this for the last sixty some years we've been in existence; let's try something different."

After that, Lynda and I took everything to the board first—get their approval because the board can give him directions on this is the way we were gonna go. I just decided to circumvent him altogether and let the board deal with him. Later on, Lynda and I had a meeting with the staff and were informed that the staff was actually developing strategies for achieving this goal and some plan of action. I reserve judgment on that, because I just haven't been there to see for myself. And also I don't have privy to all of their staff meetings.

Yuri: Tell me more about your interactions with the board.

P.K.: Prior to my leaving, I had a lot of conversations with the board. At the time, I felt very good about the new board that was coming in and the commitment from them to work directly with us approving and reaching this goal. I did have a very favorable response, and I think there was a sincere commitment on the part of the board to making it happen, especially with the incoming president.

Yuri: What happened to the diversity movement after you left?

P.K.: It's still in process. The remaining leader and I have regular conversations, and she bounces ideas off of me. I try not to influence her decisions too much or to plant too many seeds, but it's kind of difficult not to because diversity at UUFR is near and dear to my heart. But I guess it would be fair to say I haven't made a decision about what I'm gonna do. Maybe I'm just taking a break. Maybe I'm just taking a sabbatical, kind of readjusting, recalibrating my thought process. But when I'm gonna make my transition, I want to go back and have my name carved on a stone in their memorial garden. I'm hopeful that UUFR can become the shining light upon a hill even if I'm not there. I think that the community at large and UUFR as a congregation would be better served if they'll continue to expand toward a diversity that takes in consideration all the people who are living around the area in which it serves.

Yuri: Thank you very much for sharing your stories.

Eavesdropping—5

I'm tired of people asking me where I am from.
I don't like people telling me that I speak good English. I really hate
people telling me that my US-born children speak excellent English.

Eavesdropping—6

I don't have a very high expectation for my congregation.
I just go there to get inspired by good speakers,
attend some meetings, and then go home.

Coming Full Circle: My Journey with Unitarian Universalism

Yuri Yamamoto

"Yuri, I don't see you as a person of color!"

A dear white Unitarian Universalist friend of mine came up to me with a big smile. Clearly she meant this as a compliment. Perhaps she meant I was one of them, she didn't discriminate me, she didn't see my color... Or did she mean that she just saw me as Yuri, her friend? She appeared to be full of joy and hope, and probably was ready to give me a big hug, too.

Having already been in a bad mood, I had a violent reaction.

"That makes me feel invisible!"

I totally lost it. Torn between my raw emotions and trying to be a loving person informed by Unitarian Universalism, I felt my facial muscles tighten in every which way while throwing random questions at her. My friend looked bewildered. She explained how she had grown up in California with lots of Japanese American friends whom she considered a part of her community. She did not know many black people, so she wanted to meet them...

I stopped listening to her. I brought up the Japanese internment camps during the World War II that must have affected families of her Japanese American friends. She said that her friends never seemed to have been affected by their families' experiences from the horrific history. I replied,

"Perhaps they just didn't tell you?"

There was a silence and then a gasp.

"Oh, my gosh, I never thought of that."

Tears rolled down her cheeks.

We had just finished a weekend conference with representatives from several congregations committed to the journey toward multiculturalism. I had been feeling progressively worse during the conference because conversations were totally focused on the black-and-white dichotomy. There appeared to be very few, if any, yellow faces in the room other than me. Furthermore, some presenters sounded self-congratulatory about their accomplishments while pointing fingers at those absent from the room. There was no time for self-reflection and anti-racism work on our own.

How typical for Unitarian Universalists, I thought as my disappointment grew.

My experiences with Unitarian Universalism in the last thirteen years include both frustrations like this and rich opportunities to learn, grow, and love. *It is just like life,* I try to tell myself, but I keep finding myself on the fence about this faith.

Growing Up in Japan

I was born in 1960 and was raised as an only child of two former revolutionaries in Tokyo.

When I was in the first grade, a stranger molested me in a park bathroom. I did not understand what he had done to me, but my mother's reaction to my story revealed that something very bad had happened. I was convinced that she had not believed it. The man continued to stalk me afterward, but I never told anyone about it.

I became an angry child. I desperately hated being a girl. While my girlfriends were dreaming about becoming brides, I declared never to marry. I rejected everything about my mother, and she became the model of what I loathed to become.

I was very unhappy to be a Japanese, too. I could not submit myself to the cultural and social expectations of how one should behave and succeed. Most men regarded women as their servants or objects of their desire, and there were very few career opportunities for women. It was suffocating. I was terribly ashamed of the atrocities committed by the Japanese against humanity before and during the World War II, and how they still looked down on Asians while sucking up to white people.

I loved beautiful ocean, mountains and farms, old temples and shrines, traditional literature, performing arts, festivals and artworks in Japan. But Japan was destroying them with construction that altered the landscapes, horrible pollution, consumerism, political corruptions, and an insatiable obsession with Euro-American cultures.

The world was a dirty and ugly place, and I was at its center, becoming dirtier every day.

I was a voracious reader, especially interested in the dark side of humanity. I admired stories and writings of people who died young, including those who had the courage to terminate their own lives.

I started piano lessons when I was three years old. I never enjoyed practicing the piano, but my sight-reading skills and quick memorization abilities kept me ahead of other students for many years. As I became older, I began having a hard time keeping up with piano lessons. One day, a famous professor informed me that I was not competitive or hard-working enough to be accepted by a prestigious conservatory. I was too proud to apply for other schools, and sadly, did not see how I could enjoy playing the piano on my own.

Defeated, I quit piano lessons when I was eighteen. My love for music continued, but I was afraid to touch the piano to face my deteriorating skills.

I listened to music to get away from the reality. I remember listening to Dvorak's *New World Symphony* or Bach's *Toccata and Fugue in D minor* for hours until I memorized the tunes. I eagerly waited for Simon and Garfunkel, the Carpenters, or Stevie Wonder on a midnight radio show and tried to understand the lyrics on the record jackets with my English-Japanese dictionary. Melancholic Japanese *enka* songs about lost love resonated with me long before I lost—or even had—any love.

It took me over ten years before I started playing the piano again.

Nascent Spirituality

While growing up, I had no appreciation for religious organizations. A traditional Japanese family typically belonged to a Shinto shrine and a Buddhist temple simultaneously. Most Japanese practiced some rituals related to both traditions. Ceremonies for the newborn, children at ages three, five, and seven, and marriage were usually performed in Shinto styles; everything related to death and ancestors was handled by Buddhist temples. A traditional family usually had both Shinto and Buddhist altars in their home for performing daily rituals.

Most people seemed to participate in these cultural practices out of habit or a sense of duty without deep spiritual meaning. The Japanese appeared more interested in asking various gods to help with their problems in life, like college entrance exams, job hunting, or finding a good spouse. During the New Year celebration, many people visited temples and shrines to give money and pray for a healthy, prosperous, and successful year.

Christianity, on the other hand, was oppressed for hundreds of years in Japan. Even in the late twentieth century, Christians were few and far between in Japan and seemed more committed to their faith, either because they chose it for the message of love and justice or their ancestors hid their faith for centuries. When I was growing up, Christianity was legal but mostly viewed as foreign or exotic, and Christians were often discriminated against.

My parents were staunch anti-authoritarians, were non-religious—perhaps anti-religious would be more accurate—and viewed religious organizations with skepticisms because they often aligned themselves with power or exercised their own power to control people. My paternal ancestors were Shinto priests for generations, but my father detested all rituals, including weddings and funerals.

Yet I was strangely drawn to the cultural and religious practices and teachings of Buddhism and Shintoism, which have coexisted in Japan for more than a thousand years. Standing alone in the lush green forest or looking out to the roaring grey ocean in the harsh winter, I felt the presence of the *yao-yorozu-no-kami*, or eight million gods, of Shintoism. The possibility of having previous and future lives through reincarnation fascinated me, and Buddhist chants and bells soothed my heart. The idea of living alone in a little cave in a remote mountain or a communal life at a monastery attracted me.

When I was a teen, I developed a set of beliefs: there was a unique god in me and in each person; when someone claimed to have heard a god's voice, it actually came from the god within her; even though each god was unique, most people preferred to share their god with others, because believing in a universal god made them feel more confident and secure about themselves; those who did not hear any god's voice followed a confident leader or a group because they also wanted the sense of security.

I preferred to be a lone seeker and looked down on the weak people who congregated for comfort. I visited many shrines and temples and walked alone in the mountains and on the deserted beaches to seek gods who might help me hear my own god's voice. This kind of practice, to me, was the true path to spirituality and enlightenment that ancient seekers had written about.

I am not sure if I ever heard any god's voice, let alone my own. My world was very simple then, pretty much divided into black and white according to my own standards. I felt sufficient without any faith community.

Coming to *Amerika*

When I was studying animal science as the only female student with twenty-eight classmates at the University of Kyoto, no professional jobs were available for women, and most professors—all male—were unsympathetic to female students. My adviser, a rare sympathetic male, encouraged me to come to *Amerika*—as we call the United States in Japan—for better education and opportunity.

After college, I went to study at National Institute of Genetics where I met a postdoctoral scientist who was soon coming to *Amerika* as a visiting researcher. I was attracted to him on the first sight and wanted to follow. We got married in 1983 by transpacific mail so I could join him in North Carolina.

After coming to *Amerika* in 1984, I studied genetics at North Carolina State University and received a PhD in 1990. In Japan, I had been severely discriminated as a female. But in the United States, I had an equal chance if I became a real American, I thought. I was determined to learn English and succeed in my career as a scientist.

In those days, science was my omnipotent God to objectively answer all questions about the world. I turned away from the god in my heart and gods around me.

Doubts

When I arrived at my congregation in 2003, my blind faith in science was long gone.

My specialty of plant genetic engineering had become embroiled in a debate over the commercialization of genetically modified organisms (GMO) for food production. Some scientists joined political camps to claim that the GMO would either save or destroy the world. I could not understand why any conscientious scientists would make such blanket statements with certainty when we had little knowledge about the complex science behind the technology and the world around it.

The controversy opened my eyes to the nature of science as a human endeavor with dirty politics and greed instead of what I had believed to be the objective search for truth. I began to see how science was used in our society to control people, just like religions had been for centuries. Disgusted, I lost faith in science and left my job.

When I was wrestling with the uncertainties of my future in 2003, a university friend called me about a church pianist job. This was my first encounter with Unitarian Universalism. At my job interview with Rev. Julie, I was feeling a little flip and asked her what she thought I would get from the job, aside from the salary and the Sunday morning performance opportunity.

"Well, you get to hear a free sermon every Sunday," she quipped back, and we both laughed. I had never needed a church before, and her comment sounded just silly. I had no idea how Unitarian Universalism would change my life.

Shortly after I started working at my congregation, I received a summer residency scholarship to explore the nature of science with a group of philosophers and a one-year grant to conduct research on the intersection of science and politics. For this research, I interviewed over thirty academic scientists, foresters, environmental advocates, and others to learn how they had worked together to study a controversial forest management issue.

These opportunities helped me see multiple individual truths in an issue and how a group of stakeholders with opposing interests and a multidisciplinary group of scientists could construct a collective truth from widely divergent individual truths. I developed new respect for science as a useful human enterprise with much ingenuity, intuition, hard work, and collaboration.

My new understanding of science shed light on the value of religious organizations as well. As scientific truth-seeking could be enhanced by a diverse group of participants, gathering with other seekers could enrich and deepen our understanding of religious truths. One person's truth was not enough to tell the whole story.

My world, once neatly compartmentalized into black and white, began to collapse, and many more colors started shining and interacting with each other in the cracks.

It was fortuitous that I was working at a Unitarian Universalist congregation during this monumental transition in my life. The Sunday sermons were inspiring, and I often took notes and delved deeper to learn more.

Marriage Equality

Rev. Julie's most profound sermon was about marriage equality.

I was a life-long opponent of the institution of marriage. In Japan, a traditional marriage was a duty for the sake of family ties and procreation, little to do with individuals' love or freedom. Why would any woman want to marry a man and become his lifelong servant? In my opinion, the most ideal relationship for a loving couple was an equal partnership without any legal and social bondage called marriage.

My anti-marriage opinion did not change even after I got married in 1983. I married my husband only because he had presented the immediate benefits—a dependent visa and health insurance—without mentioning a long-term commitment. We loved—and still love—each other, but I had always viewed our marriage as a compromise to the ideal.

On the day of Rev. Julie's marriage equality sermon, I was still quietly wondering why gays and lesbians could not be satisfied by getting a few legal benefits that married couples enjoyed. Rev. Julie immediately dispelled my ignorant notion: heterosexual couples were entitled to more than one thousand benefits by simply getting married. She also said that people marry for many different reasons, including love and convenience. Something melted in my heart, and I could forgive myself for breaking my vow. After that, I had no reason to oppose other peoples' wishes to marry.

Years later, I reflected on how I had benefited from our marriage beyond my imagination. I had not only built a large family with my loving husband and six children, but also occasionally enjoyed treating him as my servant!

Evolution as a Musician

After Rev. Julie left, two interim ministers came. They constantly asked us who we were and who we wanted to be. Because I was at a crossroad between two careers—science and music—I welcomed these questions. I was also transitioning from relying on science as my only faith to exploring and reclaiming a much broader array of spiritual practices. I enjoyed hearing and imagining what we could become and what my role could be in the renewed congregation.

Totally oblivious to the chaos of interim ministry around me, I was rapidly growing as a musician. When I applied for the pianist job, I am certain that my technical skills and dexterity impressed the hiring team. But complicating, fast music did not move peoples' hearts. When

I played slow, beautiful music, tears came to their eyes. I was discovering the power of music and wanted to become more effective.

As my style and my role in the congregation continue to evolve over the next twelve years, I could feel the congregation's responses changing. Today, as a music director, I work closely with other leaders to program diverse materials for Sunday worship, workshops, and other events. My broader musical language resonates with more people in the congregation, and music has become my own voice.

The Chaos

During an interim ministry year, a colleague mentioned that the way our leaders treated the staff was a violation of Unitarian Universalist principles. Her argument made sense, and I suddenly became aware of the chaos around me.

Until that day, I had assumed that all Unitarian Universalist leaders, at least ministers and religious educators, were and should be the perfect embodiments of the Unitarian Universalist principles. Otherwise, how could they lead others to become true Unitarian Universalists?

The notion that Unitarian Universalist leaders could violate their own principles troubled me. Since I was not a committed Unitarian Universalist, I felt entitled to criticize the hypocrisies and incompetency of those Unitarian Universalist leaders without examining my own behaviors and attitudes.

I could not trust them any longer and was quickly swallowed up by the chaos. In the following several years, there were many conflicts and resignations. I participated in some of the conflicts, sometimes self-righteously pointing my finger at others—but never at myself—for violating Unitarian Universalist principles.

I knew that a conflict was an opportunity for new learning and that good communication and trust were keys to resolving a conflict. But it was hard to rebuild lost trust and restore communication. I struggled in the dark just to keep myself afloat.

I felt that Unitarian Universalism had failed to guide us in good employment practices and proactive collaborative decision-making. Instead of transparency, we often practiced secrecy. I was deeply disappointed by Unitarian Universalists because they often did not behave like one.

Many years had to pass before I finally recognized my own part in this chaos and began the process of healing.

Identity Crisis

The year 2011 was an epic year for me in many ways. In March, a huge earthquake and tsunami hit Japan, followed by explosions at a nuclear plant. I was totally shaken up by the disaster and could hardly think of anything but people in Japan.

I was baffled by my sudden obsession with the country I had left behind. Since I came to *Amerika*, I had been eager to assimilate, trying to speak like a real American and to succeed in my career. Until the disaster, I seldom visited Japan.

The quest to become a real American accelerated once I started working at my congregation, where I was one of the few people of color. I remember telling others that because I could not see my own face I did not recognize my color. That others might have seen my color did not even cross my mind.

When I was still dealing with my overwhelming compassion toward Japan in June of 2011, I attended the Unitarian Universalist Association General Assembly (GA) in Charlotte, North Carolina. This was my first GA, and I was mesmerized and disoriented by the sea of white people in the middle of that multicultural southern city. It was surreal.

For some reason, I sought out multiculturalism presentations at the GA. At a workshop led by the Diverse and Revolutionary Unitarian Universalist Multicultural Ministries (DRUUMM) I felt comforted by the sight of many people of color and was disappointed that no one from my congregation was there. At the workshop I saw a Chinese-American woman cry as she described her experiences of racism at her church. In a flash, I saw my color. It was as though she had thrown an invisible wire that connected me to her.

My world turned upside down. I did not know what to do with my newly discovered identity. I realized that I had been trying to become white, and I did not want to do that anymore. I hung out at the DRUUMM booth to be with other Asian Americans. I did not know if I could tolerate my congregation anymore.

When I came back to my congregation, I was relieved to see individual faces with hearts and minds instead of a group of nameless white people. I hugged many of them and felt at home. But my identity as a person of color was permanently ingrained in me.

Prior to the GA, I had been trying to assimilate myself to the congregation—majority white, mostly older, politically liberal but not radical, well educated, and comfortable—so that I could cater to their needs. The pressure to assimilate was strong but not overt or conscious, and if there was any discomfort, I interpreted it as my own incompetence or ignorance as an immigrant.

With my newly recognized identity as a person of color, I have become much more skeptical of Unitarian Universalist "facts." For example, I have been lovingly told that *everyone* loved and knew American folk/resistance songs from the sixties and the seventies in Unitarian Universalist circles, and that I was the only one who did not know them. I felt guilty for not sharing this purportedly universal American experience and tried hard to learn them. It turned out, however, that young people, some people of color, and immigrants like me did not always know or love these songs.

I had also been told that Unitarian Universalists hated organ music and do not care for traditional sacred music. These sweeping assertions also turned out to be inaccurate.

Defining "us" as a monolithic group with a certain set of characteristics can lead to exclusive practices. While most members may feel pampered and cozy in such an environment, minorities and newcomers, especially those who do not share the characteristics, would feel alienated and marginalized. After the identity crisis, I understood the problem and how I had taken part in perpetuating these myths.

Revelation

In the spring of 2012, I was invited to attend a retreat for Unitarian Universalist professionals of color, Finding Our Way Home, in New Orleans. In the room with no white people, I felt freed from the pressure to assimilate to the majority.

This was my first chance to talk openly with Unitarian Universalist ministers and religious educators about our joys and challenges. We laughed and cried together about our own shortcomings and triumphs in our mostly white congregations.

Thanks to this retreat, for the first time I saw Unitarian Universalist ministers and educators as human beings just like me. They were on their own spiritual journeys and led the congregation by walking with them, sometimes ahead, sometimes beside, and perhaps even behind or against at times.

After that retreat, I became much more compassionate toward Unitarian Universalist leaders. This revelation and my new listening ears helped me understand my past experiences during the years of chaos. I found that I had often been embarrassingly wrong about other people. I am grateful for this Finding Our Way Home community for opening my heart.

A Unitarian Universalist of Color in Progress

For a long time, I was hesitant to call myself a Unitarian Universalist. This is in part due to the demographics. But also staying as an observer while reaping all the benefits of sermons and learning opportunities kept me in a safe place where I would not have to struggle for my own integrity and authenticity as a person of color in this overwhelmingly white denomination. And—to be honest—I could stay away from examining my baggage full of prejudice, guilt, anger, and ego.

I often feel that I would join a Unitarian Universalist congregation of color if there were one. In fact, in some difficult moments, I go to the online community of color for safety, support and encouragement. Such a community is definitely necessary as a refuge. It is not, however, a true solution to the task our principles call for. A beloved community must include all people, not just people of color or close friends.

To me, a beloved community means a sanctuary where all of us can express ourselves authentically and celebrate who we are without the fear of rejection. It is not a place where only like-minded people gather or where everyone is simply nice to each other by withholding their feelings and opinions. In a beloved community, we are committed to candid conversation and love *because of* our many—and sometimes painful—differences.

The road to build such a community is extremely long and rocky. It may be a never-ending process rather than an attainable goal. I do get bogged down from time to time.

When a liberal, justice-minded white person speaks as though privilege belongs to someone else, I get sick in my stomach. When a white person says that we should not focus on skin color, I feel diminished. On these occasions, I try to remind myself that I never recognized my privilege as a Japanese living in Japan and that I still have a lot of work to do as a guilt-ridden member of the former colonizer and aggressor.

This is very hard work, and I wish there were more people of color and white allies so that the burden would not be on just a small group of people.

Writing this essay made me realize that Unitarian Universalism and Unitarian Universalists have changed my life many times. Indeed, I can no longer talk about myself without mentioning Unitarian Universalism. There are many issues to be resolved within myself and within this denomination, but I am willing to do the work.

I am a Unitarian Universalist of Color in Progress. I truly love my friends in the Unitarian Universalists of color community and a great many white Unitarian Universalists. I am in progress toward accepting more people into my sphere of love. When I am no longer overwhelmed by "the sea of nameless white people," I truly will embrace myself as a Unitarian Universalist.

Coming Full Circle

There is a unique god in me and in each person.

I once was a lone seeker in the bleak world of black and white.

Today I embrace my insufficiency and admit that I am in need of a community.

I want to hear your god's voice as well as my own so that we can sing together.

I see the world filled with all colors inviting us to create deeper connections with my own heart, with the community, and with everything known and unknown.

Finding Home in a White Faith

Latoya Brooks

I am a Black woman! I am a Unitarian Universalist by choice. I was raised and christened in the Methodist Church and attended African Methodist Zion services with my mother. I was educated in a Catholic school from first grade until high school. My mother passed away when I was sixteen, and I separated from God altogether. As an adult, I tried on Baptist shoes, but they did not fit comfortably. I came to Unitarian Universalism because my soul could not justify exclusion and discrimination within religious communities.

As I reflected on my spiritual journey into Unitarian Universalism, I struggled to see the significance of my story—not because my story lacks relevance, but because at times I feel disconnected to the Unitarian Universalist faith. Being a Black person and seeing other Black Unitarian Universalists are far and few between.

My education and career as a sexuality educator and social worker go hand in hand with my development as a Unitarian Universalist. Before knowing the faith of Unitarian Universalism, I became familiar with Our Whole Lives, the comprehensive sexuality education curriculum published by UUA. As a sexuality educator for a teen pregnancy prevention program in New York City, I reviewed curricula and was struck that such a progressive religious community existed. In my experience as a Black woman, Black people don't talk about sex. In the words of my aunt, "Good girls keep their legs and mouths closed about sex." I knew from viewing the curricula and talking to a few Unitarian Universalists at work that I was interested in learning more about the faith. It would not be until I moved to Pennsylvania that I would branch out to explore this faith.

Like Home

In Pennsylvania, while working on my doctorate in human sexuality, I met several White Unitarian Universalists and began to visit churches in Delaware County and the Philadelphia area. The first church I visited was the Unitarian Universalist Church of Delaware County. It was not a good fit for me. While I felt welcomed, one of the members preceded to question me regarding which side of the "tracks" I lived on. I informed him that I was from New York City, and I was unaware of the city being cultural divide. Feeling welcomed yet "othered," I did not return to that church.

I eventually found my way to the Unitarian Universalist Church of the Restoration in Philadelphia. That church truly felt like home. It had a diverse mix of cultures, sexual orientations, family constellations, ethnicities, and spiritual communities coexisting in one congregation. When I looked around the church, I saw that I wasn't the only Black person and I wasn't the only person of color. That was important to me, because I did not want to feel exotic or objectified.

What drew me to joining the church was the minister at the time, a Black gay man. He seemed to be from a Christian tradition, yet he celebrated other spiritual traditions effortlessly. I loved seeing someone who looked like me. I didn't feel "othered" or like an outsider. I felt empowered seeing him in a position of power and spiritual leadership in a faith tradition that has few ministers of color.

His presence reminded me of worshipping at a traditional Black church. I also met with him for spiritual guidance just like at a traditional Black church. Him being openly gay was refreshing because it reminded me of the close-mindedness of the Black church that I did not want to affiliate with.

Soon after I joined the Church of the Restoration, my beloved minister informed the congregation that he was leaving. After he separated from the congregation, I attended a few services, but it never quite felt like home. I eventually moved to Mississippi.

Having a Black minster as part of my Unitarian Universalist journey was important for me to feel connected to the faith. During my tenure at the Church of the Restoration, I felt like I could be myself. I did not have to perform stereotypical roles bestowed upon Black people. It was not assumed that I wanted to sing in the choir, and no one tried to place me on the diversity committee.

I do not mind being asked if I wanted to sing in the choir or serve on the diversity committee, but that conversation can feel like the perpetuation of stereotypical myths, such as all Black people can sing. When I was the only person of color asked to serve on the diversity committee, it seemed my selection was just to give credibility by having a person of color present. With the Black minister, I had felt that I could serve on the diversity committee because I wanted to, not because I was fetishized or put in a box. Unitarian Universalism is a faith guided by principles that encourage us to embrace diversity and welcome all who seek to understand our spiritual traditions. Yet true diversity is lacking, so how can we truly test how welcoming we are?

The Land of Cotton, and Persecution as a Unitarian Universalist

I moved to Mississippi for work not long after separating from the Church of the Restoration. I knew very little about my new home except for its history of racism and injustice; but I figured if it had any Unitarian Universalist churches or fellowships, I would be in good hands.

Church is an integral part of Mississippi culture. As part of small talk, native Mississippians would inquire about the church I attended. I lived in Mississippi for four years and joined or befriended several congregations during my time there. When I told people I attended a Unitarian Universalist Church, most said they did not have anything like that in their town. When I informed them that there was a Unitarian Universalist congregation in town, I typically was not pressed into attending their home church. Most of the time I was not hassled; I believe that's because very few people understand what Unitarian Universalism is, and they were just glad I attended church.

When I landed in Mississippi, I attended Hattiesburg Unitarian Universalist Fellowship (HUUF) the Sunday after I arrived. It is in southern Mississippi. The fellowship community was truly welcoming. From the moment I walked in, I received hugs and handshakes and genuine interest in who I was. While there was a very small Black community that attended the fellowship, I never felt "othered" or like an outsider. The community was small with a good mix of local university professors, artists, lawyers, and other transplants to the Hattiesburg area.

Being able to attend HUUF allowed me to integrate my spiritual and political self into a safe, nurturing environment. Most members were liberal and Democrat. While race was important to me, in Mississippi I shifted from looking for Black members who looked like me to seeking members and experiences that supported my values as a liberal and a Democrat. I felt so welcomed and comfortable at HUUF, I decided to join the fellowship. But soon after I moved to Tupelo, Mississippi.

The Unitarian Universalist Congregation of Tupelo in northeast Mississippi was also a wonderful experience. The congregation was very small and met in a Jewish synagogue. As a friend of the congregation, I saw very few if any Black people in attendance. Regardless, I again felt welcomed into the congregation. Members took a genuine interest in who I was as an individual. During coffee hour, people engaged me in warm dialogue. I was also invited to attend activities outside of church.

The most important part for me was that when I did not attend, people genuinely were concerned and reached out to me. The lay minister was passionate about gay, lesbian, bisexual, and transgender people in the state of Mississippi. I was able to be involved in Give Hate a Holiday and put my social work knowledge to work with my spiritual beliefs. The Congregation of Tupelo was the second time I truly felt at home as a Unitarian Universalist.

I left my beloved home of Tupelo to move to Oxford, Mississippi, to be closer to my department. It took me a while to visit the Unitarian Universalist Congregation of Oxford. I had heard many positive things about them, and I was excited to attend. My first visit consisted of my husband and me attending the church on Easter Sunday. Welcomers at the door who engaged us in small talk cordially greeted us. As we took our seats, a woman came over and introduced herself to us. Her small talk was like an inquisition of our pedigrees, educational attainment, how we found the church, and what we were doing there.

The service was spiritually meaningful for an Easter Sunday. During the Joys and Concerns portion of the service, the same woman asked for prayer for her son, who worked around "dirty, disgusting people who leech off good citizens in the world." Some members of the congregation asked her to be mindful of her language, but she continued. The damage was done. My husband and I looked around the church and saw that we were the only Black family, and we felt uncomfortable and unwelcomed. A month or so after we attended the service, we received a welcome card. But we felt so isolated and "othered," we did not return.

My final experience as a Black Unitarian Universalist in Mississippi came the day before we were planning to move to North Carolina. My experience with the Black church in Mississippi had been very conflicting for me. I wanted to be around my people, people who looked like me, but the values and beliefs I hold did not fit with the Black church any longer.

A Black coworker asked me on my last day how I got along with the Black community during my time in Mississippi. I told him that because I did not attend a Black church, I did not feel as connected to the community. He inquired about the church I attended, and I proudly told him I am a Unitarian Universalist. Our pleasant conversation turned south. He told me he was a minister and that I should have told him sooner so he could pray over me. I explained our principles and our ability to coexist with other spiritual communities. He proceeded to condemn me to hell because I did not embrace Jesus as the one true Savior and the Holy Bible as the only true Word of God.

I am still learning how to navigate being a Unitarian Universalist and Black within the Black community. I am also learning to find safe space and create a home within the largely White faith tradition. As I navigate the world of Unitarian Universalism and Blackness, and as the Seven Principles guide my spiritual path, I am comforted by the love of our perfectly imperfect faith that seeks to welcome all people with understanding and with advocacy of human rights.

Eavesdropping—7

Last year a man thought it was funny to wear a
Mexican costume and fake a Spanish accent at a UU
Latin fundraiser in a room full of white people.
I find it hurtful when a white person dresses as a person
from an oppressed race, especially if such race is painfully
underrepresented as part of the group or event.
I wrote an email to the minister.
The minister replied in a kind and understanding
way and she will address it with the board.
Since then, we have started a lot of racism
and Black Lives Matter dialogues.
I am very proud of this group and our minister's support.

Untitled

Takiyah Nur Amin

Snapshot: High School

I was a freshman at City Honors School in Buffalo New York. I was sitting in the cafeteria with friends one day, talking about religion. Many of my friends had been raised in families where the religious tradition was singular. I knew I was different: my family was multifaith.

I grew up very close to my maternal grandparents. My lovely grandmother was a member of an African Methodist Episcopal church that she attended until her death. My grandfather, on the other hand, was a member at a very prominent Baptist church in our city. While my parents had been raised in Christian homes, they'd joined the Nation of Islam in the late sixties, during the height of the Black Power movement in the United States. By the time I was born in the late 1970s, my parents had left the Nation for a more progressive mosque.

I'd come to realize over the years that many people feel that multifaith families are bad or wrong. And my high school "friends" let me know that I was unfit to be a Christian and that my parents were likely going to hell. Or they said that because of my extroverted expression, I couldn't be a "good Muslim girl."

That day in the cafeteria, all of those feelings of being wrong or different because of my background bubbled to the surface. As I listened to my friends talk about how comfortable they felt in their faith communities and how sure they were of their beliefs, I felt myself shrinking on the inside, because I had questions—about God, about faith, about right and wrong. I longed for a community where I could live out the fullness of what I believed and be encouraged to learn new things. I wanted to be someplace that didn't make me give up the best of what I'd gotten from my parents' and grandparents' traditions.

I was bold enough to share those feelings with my friends, who promptly let me know that we didn't share the same feelings or needs. More than anything, they made me feel that my desire to be in a diverse, welcoming community that heard the voice of the divine in many sources was problematic and that I was wrong.

As I walked back to class, a young white boy with glasses and dark hair walked up to me to let me know he'd overheard me talking in the cafeteria about religion and faith. He told me I should visit the church where his father was the minister—some church with a really long name over on Elmwood Avenue. When I asked him why he thought it was a good idea, he just smiled and told me that a lot of the things I talked about in the cafeteria were totally welcome in his church.

I was immediately intrigued and excited. And, truthfully, we had driven past the beautiful building with the gothic architecture before, but I never really knew what it was and I certainly couldn't remember ever being there for anything. It would take me almost a month to gather the nerve to ask my mother to drop me off at that church for a visit.

When I walked into the church for the first time, I was stunned by how beautiful it was and how welcoming everyone was to me. From the very minute I walked into the building, I was greeted with smiling faces. I grabbed the program and sat in the balcony of the church. I was nervous, because I didn't see anybody who looked like me—no other young black woman—but I was excited about the possibility of finding a religious community that I could call home. As I flipped through the program, none of the language seemed to condemn anybody, so it felt promising.

As the service began and the congregation rose to sing, I stood up, too, even though I didn't know the words. There was something about the tone of the service, even that early, that felt welcoming and affirming. I began to feel at home.

I can't remember what the topic was that day, and I don't remember the name of the minister or what he preached. What I do remember is feeling like what I heard was something I made up myself; it rang true in a deep way. The idea that it was a religious community that believed that inspiration could be found not just in the pages of books but also in the core of our lived experience and that each one of us has inherent value made me feel like I was finally at home. I was comfortable. I was happy.

Then I went downstairs for the coffee hour.

As I stood there with my plastic cup of lemonade and half of a peanut-butter-and-jelly sandwich, I started to feel a little uncomfortable. Then a swarm of older white women approached me and stood around my small brown body in a semicircle. I was horrified when the women reached out to finger my hair and touch my skin. They said nice words to me, but something was off. Their enthusiastic requests that I come back to the church only matched the curiosity with which they approached me.

While I felt sure that they wanted me there, I did not like or appreciate the sense of surveillance and the liberty with which they approached my physical being. It was like they didn't need to respect me. I left the church that day with mixed feelings, and I felt certain I'd stumbled onto something beautiful.

I also felt certain that I wouldn't go back anytime soon.

Snapshot: College

During the five years I spent in undergraduate school, I thought a lot about religion and faith. It seemed really important that as I was growing up, I begin to refine for myself what the core of my beliefs were. I read a lot and took classes in philosophy, history, literature, and culture. My own perception of faith and its role in my life continued to grow and develop. I'd always believed in God and felt that was important, and I didn't feel the need to escape or run away from the Abrahamic faiths of my heritage.

I considered myself a person of faith even if I couldn't fully articulate what that faith was. I thought a lot about that experience at the UU church, but the overwhelming whiteness that I remembered in that space kept me from returning.

During that time, I read a lot about faith—specifically, Abrahamic faith traditions and traditional African religious practices. I thought a lot about my family and that, while my parents and grandparents had different religions, they had a lot in common as it related to social justice, prayer, and love. I kept up an active practice of study and contemplative prayer, but I really longed for community.

I attended my grandfather's Baptist church for a while, especially after my grandmother died. Initially I said that it was because I felt compelled to spend time with him after Grandma's passing, and that was true. But I also wanted a place to call home, a place where people cared about my faith development and their own. I wanted to be someplace where other people were wrestling heavily with theological questions. I wanted a faith home.

As much as I loved God and as much as I longed for community, I wasn't a member of any faith community during my time in college as an undergraduate. I spent some time browsing the website of the Unitarian Universalist Association. I even managed to get my hands on a few copies of *UU World* and really enjoyed what I'd read there. In my heart, I started to feel that being a Unitarian Universalist was my faith identity, even if because it was the only religion I knew that was elastic enough to wrap up the depth and breadth of my emerging beliefs and emerging questions. Still, I couldn't bring myself to go back to that church where the curiosity of the white folks had caused them to treat my physical presence disrespectfully.

Snapshot: Graduate School

By the time I got to graduate school in Blacksburg, Virginia, I was engaging the rigors of the master's program—I was pursuing an MFA in arts administration. It seemed absolutely critical that I do something to focus on growing and grounding myself as a person of faith.

Graduate school is hard in a lot of ways, not the least of which was being in an unfamiliar community and left to my own devices in terms of taking care of myself. As I adjusted to my studies at Virginia Tech, I continued to keep up with my life of prayer, study, and contemplation, but my desire for community had only intensified over the years.

I promptly went to the UUA website and searched for a congregation near me. It turned out that there was only one congregation in town, which didn't leave me much to choose if I didn't like it. By that point, I was certain that if the UU church didn't work out for me, I wasn't going to spend time as a congregant or parishioner in a more mainline denomination. After reading as much as I could about the congregation in Blacksburg, I decided I was going to attend a service.

I don't remember the details of that first service. What I do remember is the brilliant teaching and preaching of Rev. Christine Brownlee and the openness I felt after the service when congregants were invited to share their joys and concerns. As I looked around the congregation, I didn't see any other faces that looked like mine. Many of the congregants assured me that there was "another black member" and that perhaps one day we'd meet. With a heavy sigh, I decided it didn't matter to me—I was pretty sure no one was going to try to touch my hair or body without permission, since I was an adult. And since I was sure that I could protect myself if needed, I decided to continue coming to church.

Plenty of good things came out of me being a member of that congregation. I was introduced to authors like John Beuhrens, and I learned more about the structure of the Unitarian Universalist Association. I was able to participate in small-group ministry—something that has become very valuable to me as a Unitarian Universalist. I find that over the years, most of my friendships with church members have begun and grown in these small-group settings as opposed to Sunday-morning services or coffee hours.

I even became an assistant to the religious education director for a while after graduating, when I had a patchwork of part-time jobs to make ends meet. That experience led me to a much deeper understanding of how our church values children and is committed to high-quality religious education. As someone who wanted to be an educator someday, the commitment to intellectual rigor and the serious personal investigation of one's thoughts and beliefs really appealed to me. I started to feel more at home.

That's probably why I was really frustrated when, after attending the church for some time, many of the occasional visitors as well as regular church members would always ask me if I was a visitor or assume I was just passing through. Nobody was asking white folks at church if they were visitors or if it was their first time in the space – it was just assumed that their presence was regular and normative and mine wasn't. There was always some sense that perhaps I stumbled onto the church or didn't know where I was and wasn't sure that I needed to be there. I'm not sure if that was about race or gender or age or class, but the fact that it wasn't happening with regularity to my other church friends made me angry. It was as if the church was the natural home and domain of people who were unlike me and that, clearly, if I was there, I had to be "new" and "unfamiliar" to Unitarian Universalism.

The only way I knew how to manage my feelings was by continuing to read about the church and its history and trying to stay connected to denominational affairs. This served a dual purpose of informing me more about my chosen faith home but also as a reminder that the fools who treated me poorly at that congregation were not the entirety of the church.

That understanding was something I've held onto over the years, and it has become increasingly important as I grow older and more committed to this faith journey.

Snapshot: Living in Philadelphia

After five years in Virginia, I moved to Philadelphia to start my doctoral studies at Temple University. One of the first things I did when I got to Philadelphia was plan to visit all three of the Unitarian Universalist congregations there. I was excited to live someplace where there was more than one congregation to choose from. While I was sure that I could be active at the Church of the Larger Fellowship, I really longed for face-to-face connection with other community members.

I attended a service at the Unitarian Society of Germantown and ended up never seriously visiting the other two congregations over the years, though I attended special events at both Restoration and First Church. There was something about the preaching and teaching of Rev. Kent Matthies that I felt an immediate affinity with. Also, as I looked around the church, I realized this was the most diverse Unitarian Universalist congregation I'd ever seen.

It was very exciting at coffee hour to see lots of people of color, at least compared to where I was coming from. The white people I was around also seemed more comfortable with my presence and didn't treat me as an interloper or outsider. There didn't seem to be any assumption that I was in the wrong place or didn't know anything about the church. This went a long way in helping me feel welcome and in encouraging me to be active at church.

Germantown was home.

I had emergency surgery during my doctoral studies, and Rev. Matthies was there when I woke up at the hospital. I can remember my "very Muslim" mother visiting me in Philadelphia and taking her to church. She felt so pleased and welcome that when Rev. Matthies had his first child, she sent a gift all the way from Buffalo. And when preparing to defend my dissertation proposal and thinking of who I would invite, extending the invitation to my church friends was a no-brainer.

This was a place I wanted to be.

I was excited to be in a community that actively referenced the words and the lived experiences of people of color and didn't wait for a special occasion to do it. I was excited to be in conversation with white parents of children of color who were thinking diligently and consciously about raising their kids.

Germantown was home.

As a member of this church, I served as a delegate to the General Assembly and worked on the adult religious education committee. I was also invited to lead a service on Kwanzaa, the pan-African holiday. I was encouraged to bring my full self to this church, and I was glad.

It's amazing how an experience that seems so small can reshape the way you feel about a place.

In 2009, the film *Precious* had been released to theaters. As someone who was raised by an English teacher and with love for contemporary fiction, I read the book *Push,* on which the film was based. This film about the gritty life of a young African American girl and her mother living in inner-city New York resonated with me so deeply that I was both nervous and excited about the film, hoping for a faithful adaptation. I looked forward to talking to friends about it and knowing what they thought about it.

Perhaps one week after seeing the film, I went to church on a weeknight for a small-group ministry event and bumped into one of the older white gentlemen with whom I'd exchanged pleasantries after services on multiple occasions. Neither of us was especially in a hurry and began to shoot the breeze about what we'd done in the previous week. I mentioned going to see the film *Precious*, and his eyes lit up. He mentioned to me that he'd seen the film as well and really enjoyed it. I was a little surprised, admittedly because I didn't assume that he would have gone to see the film. But it was exciting to have a conversation about it with someone who'd seen it. I was open to sharing something of my experience with the film when he looked at me with a big grin and said, "It was *finally* good to see a film with the blacks not blaming everything on the white man."

I was stunned into silence. And I am someone who enjoys talking, so you can imagine just how stunned I was.

My church friend went on to recount how dysfunctional the lead character's family and home life was, and I was shocked by much of what he saw. He reiterated being so glad they didn't "blame their problems on the system" or some outside force and were "finally" taking responsibility for the status of their own lives.

I said very little. I listened. I was angry. More than that, I was sad. What made me sad was that this person who I considered a church friend was so comfortable deriding the kind of people depicted in the film that in many ways represented people from the community in which I grew up. I am someone who is only (very slowly) approaching middle class through educational attainment, and the casual derision of poor black and brown folks has come up again and again in my experiences with UU folks—many white, but people of color, too.

Under his commentary about the film was a sense that black people— and by extension, black films—are always looking for a scapegoat or way out or something on which to blame our collective circumstances. It also wasn't lost on me that much of this commentary ignored the deeply racist, deeply violent systems in the film—for example, education and social services—that had negatively impacted the lives of not only the lead character and her family but also the others in her community. It was clear what we needed was a conversation, but I could not have it then—not in my fragile and frustrated state. I tried to counter his words, but I was really hurt and really angry.

I decided after some thought to share my experience with members of the church leadership with whom I felt a sense of deep comfort and who I thought would have a better understanding of issues around race and community. I was frustrated to hear these white people in senior church leadership try to explain to me that certainly my church friend *didn't mean anything by it* and that I should pay more attention to his intention, not the impact that his words had on me.

One of my church friends invited me to have a sit-down conversation with this gentleman in which they would be willing to mediate, but after revealing their affinity for upholding his intention over the value of my feelings and perceptions, I didn't feel confident moving into that mediated conversation.

In many ways, Germantown is still home. But this experience has stayed with me over the years and confirmed once again that the messiness around race in our society shows up in our churches—especially when we least expect it.

Snapshot: Colorado Springs, Colorado

After completing my PhD in dance with a concentration in cultural studies, I taught at a small private college in Colorado Springs for one academic year. I realized that often colleges and universities are centered in what becomes the liberal hotbed of any given community, so it didn't surprise me that the UU congregation was in walking distance from the campus. I decided to visit the church, hoping to find a home during my short stint in Colorado Springs.

The minister was awesome. Rev. Nori Rost was well informed and a vocal advocate around LGBTQ issues in that community. And the church was relatively small in a way that felt good to me: not so big that people couldn't forge meaningful relationships. During my time in Colorado Springs, it was exciting to do a Kwanzaa service there and to speak at length with Nori about the possibility of pursuing ministry at some point in the future. I'd begun discerning a calling toward ministry, and I wanted to talk to her at length about the pathways to becoming a minister. After attending GA some years before, and seeing the global diversity of our movement, the possibility of contributing to it in a larger way began to take root. By this point I identified fully as a Unitarian Universalist and was actively supporting the Association, the Service Committee, and other affinity groups.

It probably shouldn't have shocked me when white visitors assumed I was merely a guest or visitor. But it did.

Here I am, standing in the fellowship hall, not holding the same color mug as the other visitors, wearing my chalice earrings, and holding my UUA tote bag. I'm always happy to chat with people after church, and so many times people join me in conversation. We'd go on for a little bit about the service and engage a little small talk, and inevitably the white person I was speaking to would say something along the lines of " So—ummm—so you must be new to church."

So as not to seem overly sensitive or defensive, I'd try to clarify their comments: what made them think that? Often, the follow-up would be something about how they'd "just assumed" I was new or that I "looked like a visitor."

They were the ones who were visiting. They were the ones who were new to UUism. They were the ones who assumed that since they hadn't seen me, I must not exist. They were the ones in shock and awe that I knew things about UUism and my way around. They were the ones who were new, and yet the stares and silly comments sent a clear message: What are you doing here? You are an interloper.

I'd usually just finished talking to them about some finer point of church life or UU history, and even in the face of that, the assumption was that I was out of place, not native to the space. And frankly, it was really beginning to piss me off.

Snapshot: Charlotte, North Carolina

When I started my tenure track position as a professor, I moved to Charlotte excited to find that the city had more than one UU congregation. Unlike my friends, many of whom were southern natives from mainline denominations, I didn't have a lot of options for a faith community. My plan was to visit both congregations in my city and then make a decision about where I wanted to be a member.

I visited the Unitarian Universalist Church of Charlotte first and actually fell in love with it. After some six weeks of going there, I realized that I never left that church without hearing something that seemed just for me or addressed my situation in life at the time. The ministry felt relevant. And there were lots of people at my new job who were also members of the congregation.

The real clincher for me was that the congregation had lots of adult religious-education offerings, something that the congregation closer to my home did not. The prospect of having an opportunity to engage in smaller ministry offerings again was very exciting to me, as this had been so critical to building friendships in church in the past.

The more things change, the more they stay the same. Indeed.

I've had the experience more often than I can relate of standing in coffee hour wearing my name tag and carrying the same color mug as the other members, and inevitably some white member will walk up and address me as the visitor, not the white person next to me who often is a guest.

I have had the experience of being asked on multiple occasions to teach a dance workshop for the church but have received far fewer invitations to share my thoughts or ideas as a Unitarian Universalist.

I've tried to stifle the eye roll when I'm in a small-group ministry setting and all the white folks around me are shocked and in awe when I relate some aspect of UU history or reference some piece of denominational affairs, as if I'd for sure be out of the loop or unfamiliar with them. The incredulous stares of "how would you know anything about that?" have come to me more times than I care to admit.

I've had the experience of trying to work with other people of color in my congregation to start a group that met the needs of nonwhite congregants. Unexpectedly, I've experienced the confusing and frustrating scenario of being in a conversation with other black and brown people who think it appropriate that our primary goal be ensuring that white congregants are comfortable and welcome at any and everything such a group might do—and that any community work we might undertake as people of faith for people of color be focused on uplifting the less desirable elements of our own community under the guise of some respectability project.

Sigh.

***

I'm a Unitarian Universalist. However, more than anything I feel fatigue when dealing with the racial politics of many of my congregational experiences. Going to church has reminded me more than anything that racism and antiblackness show up within congregational walls just as much as they do out in the world.

This makes me angry. And anxious. Church is not always a place of peace, reflection, and contemplation.

Well-meaning white people can be very exhausting to deal with.

The misrecognition of my place in the church as a member, the constant questioning of my fitness as a church member in subtle ways drives me nuts.

More frustrating than that, however, is trying to think about where in the world I would go if I couldn't be here. I don't want to go back to being a lonely girl in high school who didn't fit into any religious community. But with the lived experience of white folks operationalizing their bias and the people of color within the context of congregational life who also traffic in white supremacy and antiblackness, I am stuck many times between a rock and hard place.

Here's a secret: many of the people of color I've met in UU spaces over the years are there precisely because they don't want to be considered as people of color. They believe that acceptance by progressive, left-leaning white peers will signify that we've achieved some post-racial moment and that as long as we (meaning people of color) don't "bring it up," everything will be just fine.

Sigh.

I actually like who I am. I'm thrilled to be black. I'm proud of my heritage as a person of African descent. I love the history and culture of my people. And I'm especially proud of the ways in which black folks in particular have inflicted a particular kind of moral consciousness within the context of Unitarian Universalism. What I'm not proud of is the persistent manner in which subtle, well-meaning racism and bias shows up in the context of our church.

If things don't get better here, where in the hell am I supposed to go?

Eavesdropping—8

The other day I woke up with the idea of forming an
actual congregation of UUs of color—Sunday services
online, once a month, or once a quarter to start.
I have no idea what it will take, but I figure it could be a great
way to have people join us and create buzz in UUA while we
continue to attempt to fit in in our own congregations.
Has anyone considered that?
Here we are waiting for white people to change.
Let's start with us first!
A safe place for us first.
Then we can decide as a group who to invite.
Start small and build from there.

Why I Became and Why I Stay

Elandria Williams

I was raised in Powell/Knoxville, Tennessee, with my twin brother and parents that came from Florida and Alabama. We were first raised in the black Baptist church, which gave us solid black church foundations. However, we also were raised by parents who had Muslim friends from Palestine and Saudi Arabia, Buddhist friends, and acquaintances from all over and with different religions and ethnicities. They never lost touch with the black community but taught us to be friends and to connect with everyone.

A perfect example is that I stopped eating Oreos and gummy bears in the fifth grade because friends told me to, and so I did. They were Muslim and Hindu, and I stopped eating them because they were made of pig fat and horse hooves. That meant that when my Baptist minister said that everyone that did not believe in Jesus was going to hell, I had a major problem with that. So Dad and Mom allowed my twin and me to feel like we made the decision to become UU. Something else important: the Baptist church was an activist church and was progressive and did not say anything about marriage, abortion, and other more controversial topics. They just were not Universalist, and I needed Universalist Christianity.

The church we joined was the Tennessee Valley Unitarian Universalist Church in Knoxville. The first day we walked into the fourth-grade class, they were stomping cans to raise money to buy part of a rainforest so that it would not be deforested. After Sunday school, we went inside the sanctuary to church. All I remember thinking is that we were not just talking about the right thing to do, and the preacher is not just preaching it, but that we—even though we were kids—were participating in changing the world as well.

My church did a remarkable job of ensuring that young people felt cherished, loved, and important to the life of the church. We were involved in everything from running our cons to serving on the board to cooking and serving the fellowship dinner. When I was in high school, the Journey Toward Wholeness program was started by the Faith in Action office of the UUA. Our church decided to participate, and they wanted someone from our youth group to join the conversation. I decided to volunteer and did the multiweek program with my church members.

After the Charlotte General Assembly and the slavery/Thomas Jefferson ball debacle and failure to change the name of our district, a decision was made to create a Thomas Jefferson district transformation team after the UUA leadership transformation team was developed. I joined as a member of the team from my church and was on this team for over ten years. We ended up getting the name of the district changed to Southeast District at the next Charlotte General Assembly all those many years later.

I stayed in my faith because it is mine and because I found home, family, spiritual grounding, and fulfillment. Becoming involved and in leadership with DRUUMM nationally, C*UUYAN (Continental Unitarian Universalist Young Adult Network), Groundwork Collective (anti-racism youth and youth-adult training collective), youth and lay adult chaplain trainings, the ecumenical young adult ministry team through the National Council of Churches, and so much more has brought joy to my life.

I met many of my best friends attending my first young adult gathering in 2003. The people that touched my heart there are now ministers and religious education leaders who are changing our denomination. The young people that grew up in my church are also ministers, religious educators, and lay leaders in California, New York, Boston, Florida, Connecticut, and in the four local churches in our area.

What has allowed me to stay and what ensures that I stay is that this faith is grounded in who I am. Though I have taken breaks from the institution, that is not taking a break from the faith. No one can define for you your relationship with spirit and spiritual community, and my spiritual home and Universalist values and faith are one. That doesn't mean that I don't attend other churches and that yoga, prayer, and meditation are not essential to my life.

Being black and a person of color in this denomination hasn't always been easy, but I have found family and home, knowing that we return and return again. This is my blue boat home.

Affinity

Kamila Jacob

About ten years ago, I attended an Anti-Racism/Anti-Oppression (AR/AO) Youth CON. For our evening activity, the group was told we would pick an affinity group—white or person of color. White or person of color (POC)? I am both. How was I supposed to choose? Why was I supposed to choose? Going to the POC group felt like I would deny my whiteness, which felt like denying my mother's love, wisdom, and care. But I knew I had specific experiences as a person of color that wouldn't be understood if I went to the white affinity group.

I found myself a spot to sit alone and begin grappling with my decision. Two older youths came over to check on me. They both identified as people of color, and one of them was mixed like me. I was invited to think about how I felt, how I identified myself, and how the world identified me.

I thought about the everyday looks of confusion when my mom and I were together; her being white, it seemed baffling to many people that I was her daughter. I thought about times when my younger sister and I were asked to "please step back" as our mother paid for items in a store. Our mother then had to defend our relationship. My sister and I were speechless because why would someone question that?

How does the world identify me? I thought about my home congregation, which I attended from a young girl to the tender age of thirteen. This congregation was racially diverse and was intentional about centering many different experiences. I thought about my new congregation where I had joined the youth group. The leaders and members of my new congregation were predominantly white, and so was my youth group. This was a change for me—I became much more aware of my race. I recalled how many times I was approached because people thought I was the daughter of another woman of color in the congregation. This woman had two kids of her own who had spent years at the church already. Why did they think I was her daughter when I had just started attending?

How did the world identify me? Reflecting on these experiences, I realized I was crying—pretty hard, actually. I was crying, and my fellow youths were there for me. They were with me, acknowledging my frustration that my identity wasn't what I defined for myself. They were with me as I processed what I was constantly taking in and internalizing from the world around me. They were there for me and knew how to support me. Part of our affinity group time allowed us to be with one another, be present, and support each person's needs. We got to be connected and be heard.

As a 3rd generation Unitarian Universalist, the Seven Principles are my morals, my values, and how I live my life. The principles guide my welcoming personality, whether I have just met someone or known them for years. When someone finds UUism and feels welcome, I am happy for them. I remind them this is a religion that accepts different beliefs. This is not the same as believing whatever you want. We covenant together to affirm and promote the Seven Principles and sources; we draw from our roots and the present world we live in. This is challenging to embody. It is a practice and it is often difficult to uphold, as our values can be considered counter-culture.

We are a community that strives to support everyone. Not an easy task. We are a community that celebrates our accomplishments and acknowledges our failings—to a certain extent. What I hope is that we can push ourselves to see the need for cultural change. We can be who we say we are, and to do so we need to accept that the work doesn't stop. We can make it if we support each other.

Choosing which affinity group to join turned out to be the easy part. Reliving so many experiences of microaggressions and oppression, of feeling alone, unsupported, and confused—that was very hard. Realizing how many stories I had of these feelings happening at my own church was heartbreaking.

I hope UUs can work together to celebrate individuals in all aspects of their identity. We share principles, but not experiences for many reasons, not just because of our religious/spiritual/faith identities. My experiences are similar and different from many in my congregation because of my race, gender, gender presentation, sexual orientation, age, socioeconomic class, education, passions, hairstyle, and more. This is beautiful. It must be celebrated, and there are so many resources to help us celebrate diversity in an intentional way. Being intentional in this celebration means highlighting my experience and my pain so that I feel seen and heard and valid. The tools are there—they are here. We just have to realize that the future of UUism depends on us utilizing them. We must hold ourselves accountable to make sure all are truly welcomed, as our principles call us to do.

My UU identity has called me to work within UU organizations and churches. I have been a religious educator for only a few years now.

I have a strong passion for intergenerational engagement and youth empowerment. I cannot wait to continue living my UU values.

Section 2

Panel Discussion Workshop (June, 2015)

Panelists: Revs. Jonipher Kwong, Carlton
Elliott Smith, and Sunshine Wolfe

Book editors: Tim Hanami, Chandra Snell,
and Yuri Yamamoto (facilitator)

Yuri: Welcome to our workshop on Stories of Unitarian Universalists of Color, sponsored by the Diverse Revolutionary Unitarian Universalist Multicultural Ministries (DRUUMM: an organization of Unitarian Universalists of color). My name is Yuri Yamamoto. I'm the director of music at Unitarian Universalist Fellowship of Raleigh. I'd like to first introduce three co-editors of this book project, Tim Hanami, Chandra Snell, and myself. This project started maybe eighteen months ago out of Tim's email to a Google group for UUs of color. So I would like Tim, Chandra, and myself to tell you a little bit about what this project means to us.

Tim: The thought of writing a book came because of my past. I used to be a Christian, a Protestant. But I became an atheist because of racism. And after becoming a member of Throop Church in Pasadena, my pastor introduced me to DRUUMM, and I started to like DRUUMM. But then, after conversing with people from DRUUMM, I found out there were issues they were facing within their churches. So I said, "Hey, why not write a book? Let's do something about that so we could share the people within the UU churches the challenges we face as people of color. So that was the origin of the book, and everyone went for it. They said, "Cool. Let's do it." So that's how it began.

Chandra: I want to echo what Tim said. Writing about my experience as a person of color within the UU church has been just very enlightening for me personally and theologically, you know, just writing down my journey. You know, we all live our journeys. But something about when you see it just written down, you can—and I think that's the power of storytelling because we're able to—when we're living life, it seems kind of random, and it's only in looking back that we can discern patterns, and we can kind of make sense of things. So I was able to make sense of my walk just spiritually, just theologically, just, you know, from the act of writing it down. So that, in and of itself, I have found to be very powerful. And not only that, but just sometimes we think as individuals—that our problems are so unique. But you realize that, no, others have experienced, if not the same thing then something similar. And I also think that, in and of itself, can be very empowering. So that's kind of my take on it.

Yuri: Thank you. And again, those of you who came in recently, please do sit with someone you don't know. Thank you. And my name is Yuri. And for me, actually, like Chandra, writing my story was really revealing who I am and what my relationship with Unitarian Universalism is and also revisiting my racial identity crisis moment at the GA a few years ago. It really taught me about who I am. But also, speaking with potential contributors and also reading people's stories—for example, Tim is Japanese American, third generation, and I am first generation, which in the Japanese community means an immigrant from Japan. Our stories are totally different. So it's been really eye opening for me, and I really enjoy being able to share about our project today.

So now I'd like to introduce our panelists: Rev. Carlton Elliot Smith and Rev. Sunshine Wolfe and Rev. Jonipher Kwong. And because we are all going to be engaged in a conversation today, I'd like to go over a little bit of points in terms of how we can be together in community. When we talk among ourselves, let's take turns and then let's listen attentively and with respect. And also, please honor confidentiality. So what you hear from your fellow participants, let's not go out and say, "Well, such and such said this," and so on. And also, no judgment. And please ask for clarification, but no judgment. And assume good intentions, and also let's allow ourselves to make mistakes. Does anybody want to add to that list? Okay. Thank you.

So now I'd like to jump into some questions. We had I think thirteen stories, and the panelists have read them all. So my first question to a panelist—now I'd like Sunshine to start on this one—is what draws people of color to Unitarian Universalism?

Sunshine: The stories had all kinds of reasons, but the most common one seems to be that they liked our theology, our philosophy of being—particularly the principles—and the idea that multiple religious traditions are welcome. We had many people who felt like in their Christian communities they were not welcome to be who they are or they weren't allowed to consider other theological ideas. And we also had a number who were interfaith families and found a home in our religious tradition because their multiple faiths that they were raised with were welcome within Unitarian Universalism.

I think that a lot of people of color come to our congregations because of the hope of our social justice commitments, and we'll talk about some of the struggles with that in a little while. But I do think that there's some hope that our vision for what we can be as a people lives into what people of color need for the future of this world and for us to be able to survive as whole beings, whole spirits in this world. So I think that starts us off.

Carlton: Let's see. I just want to make sure I got the question right.

Yuri: So the question was, what draws people of color to Unitarian Universalism?

Carlton: Thank you. So, what draws? Well, what I want to do is engage just a little tiny bit with our audience here. So generally, what would you say—what would you think draws somebody to Unitarian Universalism, or what drew you as an individual, regardless of your ethnicity, into Unitarian Universalism? Maybe just to hear from five people just very briefly, just a word or two. Yes, please.

Male speaker: Suspension of judgment.

Carlton: Suspension of judgment. I would say that's one. Yes?

Female speaker: Sometimes you have to build your own identity—as a person of color. And the church is very supportive of everybody putting together their identity. So that's wonderful.

Carlton: So the ability to identify yourself for yourself. Yeah, got that. A couple more. Here.

Male speaker: But the first panelist mentioned the theological ideas, the social justice commitments.

Carlton: Okay, great. Over on this side, in the red.

Male speaker: A caring community, the theological ideas and openness.

Carlton: Caring community, theological ideals, and openness, as was mentioned before. Please, on the right.

Male speaker: My parents were agnostics in the fifties and felt social pressure to attend some church, and they picked the Unitarian.

Carlton: The pressure to attend church as agnostics, and that's how you end up as Unitarian. One more. Was there one more? Yes, in the purple.

Female speaker: I didn't have to be a theist.

Carlton: Did not have to be a theist. I think those are all similar reasons. I don't know if the panelists would agree on that. Jonipher, what do you think?

Jonipher: From what I've read, it certainly resonates that, for theological reasons, a lot of people of color find Unitarian Universalism to be liberating whether it's because they're agnostics or atheist or they just don't believe in the Trinity like they were taught growing up— perhaps similar to how Tim was sharing his story earlier. What's interesting is that when you talk to white people, the majority of the time the reason they became UUs is because of "community." And it's just a lot more difficult for people of color to find a sense of community in a predominantly white denomination. And so I do find it interesting to have that disparity in terms of motivation for how people initially encounter Unitarian Universalism.

Sunshine: I would add to that that, at least as a Native American person, I sometimes feel like I have to straddle multiple communities for all of me to be welcome. And so, for example, within Unitarian Universalism as a transgender person, as a person who has liberal theology and social mores and those kinds of things, Unitarian Universalism has been a home. Sometimes I struggle with the Native American portion of me being involved, but I see within us the greatest, most expansive welcomeness possible. And so that has been part of that homemaking is the potential for welcoming all of who we are and not just parts.

Yuri: Thank you. And just to add to that question, sometimes I have heard people say maybe Unitarian Universalism is too difficult or not appropriate for people of color. But it doesn't sound like that from your experiences and stories.

Sunshine: Yeah. If I understand what you're saying, you're talking about the idea that because of being in a historically marginalized location, there might be some more strength found in a religion that gives certainty, and that's not necessarily something that we do. But I don't think that that's the case. I think that certainly people go to religions that have an answer because they need some certainty in their lives. But I think that there's also some potential and possibility of hope when you know that your path is welcome as much as anyone else's—and a religion that really stands for community at the core of it, even if we don't always succeed. Right.

Yuri: Thank you. So now I would like you [the audience] to pair with somebody, and hopefully somebody you don't know. I would like you to share with each other what drew you to Unitarian Universalism, and you have three minutes. Thank you.

Yuri: Time is up. Let's move to the next question. Carlton, I would like you to lead this one. So what kinds of people of color are in Unitarian Universalist congregations? I mean, I realize we can never generalize this, but we heard stories, and you all have experiences.

Carlton: Who are people of color in our Unitarian Universalist congregations? I would say the word that comes to mind first is resilient. It takes a lot—and I'll just backtrack a little bit from my own personal story. I'm just thinking about having grown up in an African American United Methodist church, and there's a story or two in the book that are about people having grown up in the segregated South and how you have the black church over here and the white church over there in the same denomination, so, you know, coming from that, even though I was in post-segregation times myself. But it takes something to make a conscious choice, especially if you work in a context where your ethnic identity is already not affirmed, which is commonly the case if you're in some sort of corporate setting or non-profit setting, to make a choice to do that during the week and then go on the weekend, in your free, discretionary time, show up at a congregation where you're gonna have to do more of that same work and that same translation.

I'd say people with a high commitment to social justice who embrace the promise of Unitarian Universalism regardless of the outward sign that we have a long way to go before we are actually fulfilling on that in our communities, just given the pervasive racism, which we live and breathe from day to day. So that's what comes to mind for me in terms of like who's in the congregations.

We were talking a bit before this session started just about education levels and how there tends to be—if you were to poll your typical person of color in a Unitarian Universalist congregation—while we're known generally for a higher level of education as Unitarian Universalist, it might be like even that next level of education, if you're coming into it from African American tradition. And I guess I wanted to say just a bit about—touching on—what we were saying before about the need to believe in something outside of one's self, and some folks of color have made that transition inside of Unitarian Universalism or prior to coming to it.

And what comes to mind for me is just the legacy that we have of what I recall and what I learned in seminary as slave religion where religiosity is about having a kind of cosmic overseer on a certain level and all the implications of that, not that that's everyone's belief. I'm thinking about, you know, growing up in a household where God was referred to as the master, for example, and what the implications of that is over many generations. But it's quite a diverse group, I would say. Even within African American churches, there is often like a class divide, for example, based on where people are, and that plays out in our Unitarian Universalist congregations as well.

Jonipher: The word that comes to mind other than resilience is the word "loneliness." I feel like, oftentimes, just when people of color feel like they found a "home," there's no critical mass in that home, and there's no other family members that may necessarily look like them in that home. And so what ends up happening is there's a feeling of spiritual isolation and even spiritual homelessness in a sense of, "Where do I belong? Where can I fully express who I am without having to translate?" like Carlton mentioned. And why is it that the translation is left as the responsibility of the person of color and not the dominant culture that exists in that congregation? And so those are the kinds of questions that I noticed reading the stories.

And I think the other dichotomy is between lay people and clergy. So I have to admit that our denomination has done a terrific job over the years to build up religious professionals of color. And we've resourced this group of people with "Finding Our Way Home" and other opportunities for growth and development. Finding Our Way Home is an annual gathering which usually takes place around March in various places across the country for religious professionals of color, which includes ministers and religious education directors or musicians and administrators and other folks. It's an incredibly enriching time because every time we gather together, we find out that we're actually not alone and that the issues that we're dealing with—other religious professionals are dealing with as well. And yes, there are organizations like DRUUMM, the Diverse Revolutionary Unitarian Universalist Multicultural Ministries, but those are kind of few and far between in terms of resources that are available for lay people. So we're hoping that by lifting up these stories with the compilation of this book that that will amplify the voices and hopefully we won't feel as isolated on this journey.

Sunshine: One of the things that I found interesting is the diversity of the stories that for some people finding Unitarian Universalism was an amazing experience, and they found a perfect home. For others, well, they still identify as Unitarian Universalists; they haven't found a church home. I think that the people of color who come to our congregation, some of it depends on what they find at the church that they visit. I've been in seven congregations in the past twenty years either as a member or as a religious professional. And in two of those, there was enough critical mass of people of color, and there was such a sense of radical hospitality in the congregation that folks of color did not feel isolated.

Now, even in those churches, I personally experienced struggles as an indigenous person with misappropriation of our culture, and I've walked out of services angry and those kinds of things. And in those congregations [with critical mass], they took those as learning opportunities to fix what they were doing, to admit they had made a mistake and move forward.

In other congregations where there's only a few of us, there's oftentimes this experience of being, well, "Tell us about your African American experience," or, for example, in St. Louis after Ferguson, "Well, so what's it like being black in St. Louis?" You become this token, this symbol. And I think for the folks who choose Unitarian Universalism, regardless of the church that they go into, they come to us because they believe in the power of community, the light of love, and the strength of justice, and they want to see that in their religion. And so I agree resilience is a big factor particularly if they stay in a church that has not necessarily done its work and is treating them as a token. And I think that they come to some churches that are very welcoming or only attend churches that are very welcoming and not making them that token, because those congregations have done the work of living their values as their culture.

Yuri: Just a follow-up question, as critical mass has been mentioned a few times: Is this critical mass something that is always necessary, or does that mean we should just bring in all these people of color to our congregation, and that solves the issue?

Sunshine: Since I said it most recently, I'll respond to that—which is, again, in those churches, I'm thinking of—the congregation that I'm serving now does not have a critical mass. And the people of color in that community had felt very welcome. And then when Ferguson happened, they didn't feel welcome anymore. So I think it can be situation-dependent. I don't think you have to have a critical mass for people to feel welcome. It's about an attitude of the community. So it goes back to that, "How are we as a community? Are we talking to people because we see who we think they are? Are we talking to people because we think being in relationship with people is an amazing thing?" I think I gave the example earlier. The young adult group came out with a list of questions to ask during coffee hour and one of them was, "Rather than asking me what I do for a living, ask me what I love to do." Right? So what question are you asking? Are you asking because you think this person knows everything about being an indigenous person? I often get the "okay, so what part Native American are you?" which is the racist question. And then the "tell me all about your people" question, which is equally racist, or they say, "Let me tell you everything I know about Native people."

Male speaker: Or "your people."

Sunshine: Or "your people," right. Yeah. "Let me tell you about your people." Like, you know, I'm Seminole. I think I know about my people, right? You know, exactly, right. Instead of saying, "So, what do you love about Unitarian Universalism?" Or "Do you have any pets?" Or, you know, just the kind of normal things that you want to know about people, right?

Jonipher: Dr. King once said that eleven o'clock on Sunday mornings is the most segregated hour in America. And little has actually changed over the years. According to studies done, only about 8 percent of our churches can be considered "multicultural." So I'm kind of a numbers geek, and I wanted to know, well, out of that 8 percent, how many people of color are in those congregations or how many people are of a different ethnicity—because a predominantly black church, for example, would still be considered somewhat monocultural, right? And so, what's that magic number that would make a congregation multicultural? And the other question I asked was how many churches within Unitarian Universalism are considered multicultural?

So, of course, I went to the obvious and usual suspects like All Souls in Tulsa, Oklahoma, or All Souls in Washington, D.C., and colleagues were telling me, "We have about 20 percent or 30 percent people of color in our congregation." And so I thought, "Is that what it takes to qualify as a multicultural congregation—to get that stamp of approval that all of a sudden we've reached the promised land?" Or is it something more like what Sunshine was talking about? And suddenly, what Beth Zemsky said made a lot of sense. She said that diversity is about counting people, and inclusion is where people count.

Sunshine: Yes.

Jonipher: I thought that was a radically clear and precise distinction between what we're really going after. For those of us who are in more "monocultural" congregations, is the reason that we want to have more people of color in our congregation so that we could tell the rest of the UU world, "Hey, look at us. We're the good guys. We have this multiculturalism thing figured out"? Or is it because we realized that we can never be whole and holy and really live out our values as Unitarian Universalists if we don't figure out this multiculturalism thing, if we don't live out our principles and practice of inclusion? Is that the reason why? So, for me, what's more important is getting down to the root of it. I could care less if there's only one or two people of color in your congregation, but if culturally you are doing the work—that you're involved with the Black Lives Matter movement, for example, or you're out there building relationships in the community—that's what I care more about.

Yuri: Carlton, do you have some comments?

Carlton: So I think I appreciate the direction that Jonipher and Sunshine are pointing to in terms of the multicultural piece, and I think it's so important to get to a rationale behind it. What I fear sometimes in our congregations is exactly what Jonipher was just talking about: that the percentage of people of color in UU congregations is more about the comfort of the white people in those congregations than it is about spreading the love or being the love, if you will. And so from that standpoint, I think the standard for being a multicultural congregation and Unitarian Universalism is 20 percent. Am I remembering this correctly?

Yuri: I don't know.

Carlton: Something like that. That's quite a low threshold. I mean, that guarantees that you can be a multicultural congregation without looking anything like the global majority, right? I mean, so, that's the consideration that I have. I've been a Unitarian Universalist minister for many years now, and my observation is that in the absence of a mission that's thoroughly based on love, that's thoroughly based on being in relationship to one another, and being that we have such theological diversity, what I suspect has happened is that white culture has become the glue that holds Unitarian Universalism together. And I think the fear is that if you remove whiteness as being central to Unitarian Universalism, Unitarian Universalism could very well fall apart. So I think that's kind of like the fear that's back there, so whatever that's worth.

Yuri: Thank you. Since we were talking about what kind of people of color are in the UU congregations, I'd like to actually turn to co-editors. And then if you can just like quickly say who you are, maybe one minute or so. Would you like to go, Chandra, first?

Chandra: I've been a member of a UU church for a couple of years now. My personal background I think is very similar to a lot of UUs I talked to, whether they're people of color or otherwise. Well, my background, I come from a Christian background, was raised Christian—Church of Christ. I don't know if anyone's familiar with that. But you could call them fundamentalist, I think, evangelical/fundamentalist. And I was that for many, many years really—for most of my adult life, as a matter of fact. But then I just got to the point where I just started questioning things that I had been taught all my life, things that I had not really questioned up to that point. And I just started searching. And I just started reading and questioning.

My local UU church puts on a number of community events throughout the year, such as concerts and things of that nature, and I had actually attended a couple of those. I had picked up some literature and didn't look at it, just put it somewhere. But I kind of always had in the back of my mind maybe I should go to a service one of these days. And so one day I finally did.

Theologically, in terms of my personal beliefs right now, I find that it's a perfect fit. And a lot of times, my Christian friends and relatives don't quite get it. I say, well, I imagine, you know, UUism as being a big umbrella, and you can kind of be whatever you want. And I think oftentimes that translates to a lot of people is, well, you're nothing, you know, if you're everything. But I think for me right now, and I just think everybody's on a journey, and I just think that we all have to figure it out for ourselves.

For me at this point in my journey, I feel that the Unitarian church is a good fit. Now, that said, I'm also in the ordination process in the UMC church. That is another conversation for another time. You have to read my story. But I will say that I don't find a contradiction there. Some people would find a contradiction, but my theology is such that I don't find a contradiction. But, you know, I feel—I feel that this is a good fit for me right now.

Yuri: Thank you. Tim?

Tim: I'm Japanese. And Yuri here is Japanese, too. I'm Japanese American. Even though we're both Japanese, Yuri and me, we're like in two different worlds, to be honest with you. And to be honest with you, I'm finding a lot of happiness here in the Unitarian Universalist church, and that's because of my pastor at Throop Church in Pasadena. She made me welcome. And the church is, you know, they accommodate me, which is really great because my last denomination, the headquarters—I'll be honest with you—they were racist. The members were racist. But the UU church members are more open. And I became a member, and I'm happy. But at the same time, when I was hearing the grievances, when I hear the anger or read the anger from the book, from the letters, I said I don't want to happen what happened to me in my former denomination in this denomination. So I said yeah, we should write a book to, you know, prevent it from happening. And I'm glad I did it, because I really do love this denomination. I love the people here. And I'm glad I came here, and I'm glad I'm a member.

Yuri: Thank you. So I actually came to a UU church as staff, a pianist. I really loved it, but my path hasn't been just straight, and you can read that part in the book. But I am from Japan, and my parents were totally anti-religious. So I came from a very non-religious background but really always was seeking something spiritual. And to me, the closest thing that feels, of course, culturally is the Shintoism and the Buddhism. I consider myself a pantheist. I believe that a god resides in everybody, everything, including the ocean and the mountains. So that's who I am, and let's just put it that way because of time constraints as well. But thank you for sharing who you are.

Let's go to the next question. And this, I'd like Jonipher to take a lead. So, what kinds of challenges are there for people of color in UU congregations? I realize some of those already came out, but there are specific things mentioned in the stories, and obviously you've experienced them or heard about them yourself. And you're also welcome to mention what actually worked.

Jonipher: When I was first called to the First Unitarian Church of Honolulu four years ago, there was actually quite a bit of conversation with the search team about how I, as their newly called minister, could bring or could make the congregation more multicultural. So I'm the solution. I'm the savior. I'm the messianic figure to turn this congregation around. And one of the first articles published by the local newspaper had the headline of "The First Unitarian Church of Honolulu calls its first gay Asian minister." And my rabbi friend called me up and said, "When did you come out as openly Asian?" And I said, "Well, I needed to do something to alleviate the fears of my congregation, because when I was going around during the candidating process, I was asked the question of, 'What if we called you as our minister? Wouldn't that make our church all gay?' And I said, 'Well, wouldn't that be wonderful? We'd be the first predominantly LGBT UU congregation in our movement.' And I said, 'But the bigger question is, wouldn't that make our congregation all Asian?' And then people were like, 'Oh, my gosh. You're right!'"

The point is, people have good intentions, but the intent and the impact are not always the same. It brings me back to the question of—just because you call a leader of color, does that mean that the culture necessarily supports that? That's one question.

The other point I wanted to make in terms of a challenge is that oftentimes we UUs think we're so smart that we have the magic bullet to solve this quandary that we've been struggling for ages and ages, right? So we wanna apply a technical fix, but it's really an adaptive question that we're struggling with here. And the adaptive question has to do not with where we're coming from but where whoever it is that is walking through our doors is coming from. And the question, I bet you a million bucks that I don't have is "Is there room for me here? Do I belong here? Can I be my authentic self here? Can I be both gay and Asian and be welcome with open and loving arms?"

So until we could grapple with that question, I would suggest that we stop it with the technical fixes, that we stop it with tokenization of just putting someone on the pulpit who's a person of color or shoving them into the board or putting them in the choir even though they can't carry a tune worth their lives. You know what I'm saying? These are some of the stories that we're reading about how we turn people off. And consequently, they become the "nones." So the nones are not necessarily those who don't know about Unitarian Universalism. They're not necessarily seekers. They have found a faith that works for them. But the people in that faith—I don't know how many of you have seen that bumper sticker that says, "Jesus, save me from your followers." You know, that's kind of like, "Unitarian Universalism, save me from Unitarian Universalists," right? So how could we stop turning people away and how can we truly practice and answer the deep questions and yearnings that people come through our doors with?

Sunshine: Oh, I've been sitting with the words that Marlin Lavanhar said on Wednesday of adapting Langston Hughes what Unitarian Universalism being Unitarian Universalism again, that religion that has not been but will be. I think that we have a lot of potential. I, like many people who are historically marginalized, who have come into this religion—and I say this both as a Seminole Cherokee Lakota and European person as well as a transgender person—is I have had some crises of faith and at some point I just said, "You know what? Heck with you all. I'm staying."

That said, that's not an easy choice to make, right? And it comes with exhaustion, and it comes with despair at times, and it comes with just all kinds of frustration. But I think that what we really have to work on is just what Jonipher was saying is how do we do our own work, and how do we hear the voices of the people who are coming to us because so many have come to our churches and said, "No, thank you." Not to our values, not to our theology, not to our great vision of what can be, but because we haven't figured out that we still need to become, that we still need to do more and grow and continue.

I was teaching a class on—classism, actually. After some time of discussion, I asked the people in the circle to tell me how they felt. And the first four people went, and they all started, "Well, I think—" And we tend to do that. We tend to go to our thought place. But a lot of this welcoming has to do with being heartfelt and authentic and not just mindful but all of us mindful and spiritual and feeling and all of it. And when we get into that place is when I think we're able to embrace folks who may not be from the same culture as us and see people for who they are.

But there are too many blinders up, and those blinders are really shutting people out from coming into our communities. But there's something about the fact that we need to do those adaptive questions, saying, you know, who are we and who do we want to become and who are we welcoming and not that if we put so and so in this committee that somehow that's going to resolve our problem.

And I think we also have to be open to the knowledge that not everything is ours. As an indigenous person, what really makes me angry is every time we use a Native American chant out of context. One of my colleagues was writing a book and was fact checking a quote from the Navajo that she had used for years, and it turned it was from a John Wayne movie. And we have to be relational. You have to do your work. You have to say, "Is utilizing this allowing for more connection, or is it just making me feel good or just because I like it, I want to hear it, or is it putting me in relationship with people?

Carlton: I think in a lot of the comments that you've heard this afternoon and that I read in the drafts of the chapters for the book, there's a lot of pain around identity inside of the association both coming into it. Because if one comes into Unitarian Universalism from another tradition, you have to leave behind something that was familiar, that was comforting, and that's true of any—how many come-outers do we have in the room, in any way, shape, or form you had to come into Unitarian Universalism from someplace else? Yeah.

So I think, you know, if there's a hope that I have for it, I hope that, you know, somehow, similar to what happened for me in relationship to the struggle for immigrants of being able to make the connection through a deeper understanding of civil rights, of being America addicted to free or very, very cheap labor and playing that out over the course of many, many generations and it just so happens it's, you know, people immigrating from Central and South America who are most in the impact of that as well as people working in sweat shops in China, etc., that if we're able to translate our experience of having come out of whatever context we came out of to be Unitarian Universalists so that we might generally be able to find some place of empathy in that regard and knowing the pain of leaving something behind in order to embrace a new vision that we can connect through that.

Another challenge I think we face is also an opportunity, and that has to do with technology and the fact that fewer and fewer people are going to church on Sunday morning. So there's something new that wants to happen, but we are so thoroughly invested at this point in the traditional way of doing things of, you know—the eleven to twelve o'clock on Sunday morning when that is starting to fall away. So there's a window of opportunity. It's opening up for creating new online communities of color, if we will—different ways of gathering, small groups that might not meet on Sundays. So all of that needs to be taken into consideration as well. But it's a challenge because we are a congregationally based movement. But hopefully we'll be able to figure out some new ways of doing faith development and religious life.

Yuri: Thank you.

[Audience gets into small groups to share what each person will do to make their congregation more welcoming.]

Yuri: I have only thirty seconds for each person to say something. If you'd like to say something, please do.

Carlton: Okay. So the only thing I want to say is, there's been a mention of social justice and the importance of social justice. As a little brief announcement, I'm a part of the Southern Region staff, and I wanted to remind everyone that the July 13th action that we are doing in Winston-Salem, North Carolina, with regards to voting rights, just like little tiny flyers that are back there on the table.

Sunshine: Okay. I just kind of talk a quick story. I had my internship at West Shore Unitarian Universalist Church, and we had an organization come in and talk about doing work with immigrants in the nearby town. And one of the things that we did was the covenant in Spanish. The one that begins, "Love is the spirit of this church." We did it one week, we just added, *"El amore es el espíritu de esta iglesia,"* and we liked it so much, the ministers, we did it again. And that led to a major conflict within the congregation about whether we wanted Spanish. It led to an adaptive conversation about what it meant to be welcoming. And somebody said something horribly offensive to one of our Mexican American members of the congregation and that led to a moment of conflict and then healing. One of the things I want to add is that in all of this, don't be afraid of the conflict, engage in the learning.

Jonipher: If you look around you in this room, and throughout GA, you'll notice that we are beginning to become a more colorful denomination. So I would encourage you to keep struggling with these questions, and I'm just so glad that we're not having GA in Vegas, because what happens at GA ought not to stay at GA.

Chandra: Well, in that spirit, Jonipher, I was so touched by something that one of the speakers said in the audience, and that is sometimes, I think, just in everything that goes on, we forget that we're all human beings. We're not representatives of a group, you know. If someone says, "Oh, well, that's a white man," is that the sum total of who you are? Does that begin to describe who you are? Or you know, I'm a whatever, you know, we're all human beings, and I think a lot of times that gets lost in well-intentioned conversation. You know, and I think sometimes we just need to come back to that, how would you like to be treated and I think we have such an advantage as UUs. We have such an advantage that needs to be spread out in the larger world, because UUs do have that intention. And you can always say that about the rest of the world, and I think we ought to use that good intention to our advantage. Okay, you know, may I quote the scripture?

Yuri: Please.

Chandra: "Do unto others as you would have them do unto you." I think we can all agree with that one.

Yuri: Thank you so much for your engagement, and thanks to all the panel members.

Afterword

Teaching Hearts and Minds to Open for Multicultural Change
Mark A. Hicks, Ed.D.

MacLean Professor of Religious Education and Director, The
Fahs Collaborative Laboratory for Innovation in Faith Formation

If you told me ten weeks ago that I'd be sitting in circle with
black Christians, singing a gospel song about interconnectedness,
I would have told you that you were crazy!
White, male humanist

Thank you for telling something I didn't want to hear. You're
helping me return to the real intentions of my heart.
White, female, Jewish elder

Simply because black people know oppression does not mean we
have nothing to learn about how we've been shaped by racism.
Black, female lay leader

Writing stories about how racial truths shape our lives can be risky
business. The writer has an opportunity to empower those lurking in
the destabilizing shadows of racism to step into the light, daring to
name truths that can freeze a person into perpetual states of fear, anger,
shame. At the same time, daring to go public with a personal truth

nudges the writer toward self-healing. Together, the act of reading and writing stories of hardship creates new realities, new ways to signal to self and Other that the world they know can be otherwise.

I wrote *Beloved Conversations: Meditations on Race and Ethnicity* for reasons similar to the writer who decides to tell a risky truth. My own experience as a middle-class African American was one of paradoxes and hiding from my own truth and power. I was expected to assimilate while pushing social boundaries, to be part of DuBois's Talented Tenth, but maintain a sense of commonness.

Yet, the more I engaged across cultural lines in school, church, and the workplace, the more unsatisfying that way of life became. The socializing impulses of my youth and young adult years crystalized into conflict-avoidant ways of being, trying to please everyone, often suffering alone in isolation and confusion. When white teachers and classmates activated racist stereotypes, I remained quiet, kept my head down, relishing in that adolescent righteousness: "I'll prove my brilliance to you one day."

Thank goodness I matured, but my racial life got worse. The institutionalized system of racism beat me down. But, over time, I came to realize that my experience of double-consciousness was not unique, that my story was relevant, and even more important, that I was not to blame for the sense of incompleteness and inadequacy that seemed to be an ever-present companion. Paraphrasing the words from novelist Toni Morrison's *Beloved*: I found companions who became friends of my mind, my heart, and my sense living into a positive future.

As I moved deeper into the religious and cultural experience of Unitarian Universalism, I discovered I shared a common thread among friends and colleagues. Like me, people were compelled to name and critique how race misshaped their sense of wholeness, of justice. Folks could earn top grades doing the work of denouncing racist language, behaviors, and practices. But while quick to march or turn out a business meeting or publicly shame a wrongdoer, there was a haunting shrillness that was not softened by a spiritual core, the sense of compassion and empathy that nurtures the soul after a heart has been broken.

I began to see this everywhere. People of color—the targets of racism—often expected that spouting logical, confessional, and passionate anti-racist language would translate into new practices and ways of being. Instead, exhaustion set in, what the sociologist of education Michael Smith calls, "racial battle fatigue," where souls are murdered by a thousand cuts. People of color leave our religious community disappointed, spiritually drained, and often filled with sarcasm—even scorn—for our community. Whites, likewise disappointed by a lack of progress, sometimes leave, but, more than not, they find solace in the cultural systems of their congregation. At the very least, they might say, the system of whiteness still speaks to major needs of their lives (friendships, liturgy, music, a sense of community). As one white congregant said, exasperated by a minister of color she thought was a bad match for the congregation: "At least I still have [white minister's name], who understands me."

It is this admixture of thoughts, feelings, and emotions that calls the transformative power of religious education into action. *Beloved Conversations: Meditations on Race and Ethnicity* is a teaching and learning curriculum that holds both the tensions and the joys of an intentional multicultural* community. The curriculum assumes that every conversation with another human being is a cross-cultural conversation, even if your conversation partner is from the same cultural group. As such, it explores the social constructs of race and ethnicity as a *spiritual* exercise, allowing people to give shape to their own story while learning how to honor the experience of others. It promotes resilience, challenging everyone to hear naked truths and not run away when the truth is difficult to hear. Nested inside communities of faith, *Beloved Conversations* creates the first step—a learning laboratory—for how to live healthily in a multiracial, multicultural, and often theologically diverse community.

The curriculum differs greatly from traditional diversity workshops that suggest it is possible to "train" participants to respond to cultural differences as a matter of dos and don'ts. Matters related to the human condition are never easy to name or fully understand. There is no prescription, no magical solution that "fixes" unhealthy dispositions or personalities. That is why the curriculum invites participants into a "learning community" so they have a chance to unpack their assumptions, gently, while embedded in the robust context of cross-cultural relationships. Such a format allows for "unlearning" (Wink, 2011) patterns of thought, feelings, and emotions that contribute to walls of division. Best of all, it's all done with an eye toward the spiritual and communal commitments we hold as people of faith.

The curriculum is deeply rooted in the theoretical framework of "transformative teaching and learning" (see the writing of Jack Mezorow in Cranton, 2006), which asks learners to reflect on what really matters in their lives and provides culturally relevant learning strategies for how to achieve those aims. The curriculum uses a range of evocative teaching tools to signal a fresh approach to exploring human diversity as psycho-spiritual work. It opens with a one-and-a-half-day learning laboratory in the form of a retreat (usually a Friday evening and Saturday). The retreat explicitly models the pedagogy and spirit of the curriculum. After a learning community is formed, eight two-hour seminars are designed as follow-up sessions to help participants locate their individual and group assumptions about race and ethnicity in their lives. At the same time, learners are constantly asked to think about how social systems intersect with their personal journey.

The curriculum is experiential through and through, using music, visual arts, digital media, theater, film, and the best practices of small-group ministry to make its point. The retreat is led by an authorized staff member from the Fahs Collaborative who has deep experience in faith-based, social justice education. The eight sessions that follow the retreat are facilitated by two facilitators chosen by and from within the sponsoring congregation(s).

Beloved Conversations alone is not the magic solution to a congregation's or community's work on racial/cultural/theological diversity. It should be conceptualized as one among many tools that help faith communities reach their goal of living into the dream of our multicultural world, even if the community is "all white." Sociologists of religion (see Emerson, 2009) widely confirm that only 4 percent of congregations in the United States are multiracial, in large part because congregations lack effective teaching and learning strategies that encourage every cultural group within the congregation to grow and develop cross-cultural competencies. Thus *Beloved Conversations* serves as more than a curriculum to help members of a congregation better relate one to the other; it also helps members retune their spiritual antennae to the needs of the world already swirling around them.

The Fahs Collaborative realizes that change does not happen without thoughtful planning, spiritual discernment, and a highly relational commitment to the process of "doing the work for as long as it takes." As such, the collaborative provides professional staff support to help the congregation assess its readiness to engage. That process is followed up with individual and group coaching via digital formats (video conference, phone calls, and so forth).

Upon purchasing a license to use the curriculum, congregational leaders become members of the Beloved Conversations Network, a group of over sixty (and growing) congregations across North America who are grappling with the dynamics of shifting their personal and collective identities away from a monocultural religious practice. Because we are all still learning how to create this new vision of our world, members are expected to share their successes and struggles. Yes, it takes a village!

As you consider this resource, think about your readiness to begin.

- Has you congregation explored how its mission includes cultural diversity as one of its core commitments?

- Is your congregational leadership ready to commit its resources to supporting such a paradigm shift?

- Has your faith community considered how your theology speaks to the demands of cultural diversity? How will you minister to those in your community who are culturally dominant as well as those who have been historical targets of dominant-culture oppression?

- Has your congregation considered how your present context would make doing this work difficult at this juncture (for example, a change in leadership, a capital campaign, toxic problems that reach across all aspect of community life, geography, etc.)

- Has your congregation developed a plan of action (at least for the next sixteen months) for how it will provide ongoing teaching and learning opportunities for its members?

Our experience teaches us that answering no to any of these questions suggests intentional preliminary work needs to be considered. Clearly the need to create multiracial congregations continues to be a moral imperative for our time, but doing the work poorly causes a great deal of harm and pain for everyone. Our staff is ready and happy to speak with you about your current context; we welcome your questions.

Beloved Conversations was created in 2013. What have we learned so far? Reports from members in the network are both encouraging while challenging us to dig deeper. Congregational leaders report that people are

- more courageous in engaging in cross-cultural dialogue;

- more comfortable in taking risks to communicate deeply held assumptions about race and ethnicity;

- better equipped to sit with cultural differences;

- more adaptable in dealing with different standards of worship, music, education;

- more fluid when translating personal communication styles and theological commitments to other preferences and traditions;

- better able to link personal power to systematic oppressions;

- more resilient when confronting the status quo;

- more curious about personal, narrowly held assumptions;

- better able to set aside issues of perfectionism and judgment when encountering different standards.

In addition, people of color and folks who are often discouraged by the monocultural framework of mostly white congregations are finding ways to attend to their own faith formation, meaning, ways to name and heal around their experiences as targets of oppression both within the religious community and in society at large.

So it is that *Beloved Conversations* is making a significant difference in the lives of many of its participants. As a teaching and learning organization, we are curious to know more about how its model impacts individuals and their congregations. Researchers at the Fahs Collaborative are taking those questions seriously and is devoting time for scholarly exploration. We welcome your interest and participation in this cutting-edge work.

The Fahs Collaborative Laboratory for Innovation in Faith Formation (http://www.meadville.edu/beloved) is a faith-based, nonprofit teaching and learning organization that creates resources that spark human potential. It is the parent of Beloved Conversations. *The collaborative is hosted by Meadville Lombard Theological School, the Unitarian Universalist seminary in Chicago.*

References/Notes

Multicultural, used here, refers to social constructions of identity that can be the source of inspiration and pride or, at the same time, the source of oppression. Examples include race, ethnicity, religious tradition, gender/gender identification, sexuality, nationality, economic resources, etc.

Cranton, Patricia. 2006. *Understanding and promoting transformative learning: A guide for educators of adults.* 2nd ed. San Francisco: Jossey-Bass.

Emerson, Michael. 2008. *People of the Dream: Multi-racial congregations in the United States.* Princeton, NJ: Princeton University Press.

Wink, Joan, 2011. Critical Pedagogy: Notes from the real world. 4th ed.

Appendix

Organizations and Programs Specifically Serving Unitarian Universalists of Color

Diverse Revolutionary Unitarian Universalist Multicultural Ministries (DRUUMM) http://druumm.onefireplace.org/

Rev. Joseph Santos-Lyons (president 2015-2017)

DRUUMM is a Unitarian Universalist People of Color Ministry and anti-racist collective bringing lay and religious professionals together to overcome racism through resistance and transform Unitarian Universalism through our multicultural experiences. We developed from several older ministries, namely the African American UU Ministries and Jubilee World anti-racism change trainings.

DRUUMM has a growing membership of UU People of Color from every district and region. As an all-volunteer ministry, DRUUMM continues to lead efforts to fulfill the Journey Toward Wholeness Resolution toward becoming an anti-racist, anti-oppressive, multicultural UUA, creating space for youth, young adult, and our families of color to heal and work collectively, and stewarding an effective organization that develops new leadership and manages consistent communication with members.

Black Lives of Unitarian Universalism (BLUU)

http://www.blacklivesuu.com/

Black Lives of UU provides information, resources and support for Black Unitarian Universalists and works to expand the role & visibility of Black UUs within our faith.

Google Group and monthly online meetings of Unitarian Universalists of color

Contact: Jessica York, Faith Development Director, Unitarian Universalist Association, jyork@uua.org

Church of the Larger Fellowship (A Unitarian Universalist congregational without walls)

People of Color Covenant Group: http://www.questformeaning.org/poc-covenant-group/

Black Lives Matter: https://www.questformeaning.org/black-lives-matter/

Ministerio Latino: http://www.igcuu.org/

An Organization of Unitarian Universalist White Allies

Allies for Racial Equity (ARE), a Unitarian Universalist white allies organization in partnership with DRUUMM

http://alliesforracialequity.wildapricot.org/

History (reprinted from the ARE website with permission)

ARE began as the White Anti-Racist Allies Caucus of DRUUMM, a UU People of Color Organization. In 2005, the leadership of DRUUMM decided that a new relationship was needed between DRUUMM and its allies in order for all of us to be able to do the racial identity work that strengthens our multiracial coalitions. They requested that white allies get together to form a partner organization rather than a caucus.

In response to this request, thirty-six individuals who identified as white people committed to anti-racism work gathered in Tom's River, New Jersey, in November 2005 to develop a formal organization with a clear leadership structure. The planning team who organized the conference (Minton Brooks, Beth Dana, Julian Sharp, Annette Marquis, Hannah Stampe, Diane Martin and Gini Courter), asked the Rev. Dr. Tracey Robinson-Harris, then the Director of Congregational Services for the UUA, to facilitate the business meetings to help accomplish the ambitious goals.

By the end of the weekend, the group adopted a vision, mission, and organizational structure; affirmed DRUUMM's understanding of our relationship, adopted an organizational structure, developed a proposed list of short term and longer term objectives, elected a steering committee, and began a membership drive. The new organization was named Allies for Racial Equity.

Today, DRUUMM and ARE leadership maintain a close relationship with ongoing reporting, face-to-face meetings, and DRUUMM participation in the ARE nominating process.

Unitarian Universalist Curricula, Web Pages, and Resources on Multiculturalism and Anti-Racism (as of March, 2017)

Building the World We Dream About: A tapestry of faith program for adults by Dr. Mark A. Hicks

http://www.uua.org/re/tapestry/adults/btwwda

Examining Whiteness: An anti-racism curriculum by Rev. Dr. William Gardiner

http://www.uua.org/multiculturalism/curricula/whiteness

Beloved Conversations by Dr. Mark A. Hicks (read more about it in Afterword)

http://www.meadville.edu/beloved

Multicultural Welcome: A Resource for Greeters in Unitarian Universalist Congregations

http://www.uua.org/sites/live-new.uua.org/files/documents/idbm/multicultural_welcome.pdf

Discussion Guide for Considering the Report and Responsive Resolution from the UUA Board on the Doctrine of Discovery

http://www.uua.org/sites/live-new.uua.org/files/documents/lfd/dod_discuss_guide.pdf

Marching in the Arc of Justice Toolkit

http://www.uua.org/multiculturalism/toolkit

Discussion Guide: An Indigenous Peoples' History of the United States by Roxanne Dunbar-Ortiz (Boston: Beacon Press, 2014)

http://www.uua.org/sites/live-new.uua.org/files/documents/dunbar-ortizroxanne/discuss_guide_indigenous.pdf

Unitarian Universalist Association Racial Justice & Multicultural Ministries

http://www.uua.org/multiculturalism

Be the Change: Youth Multiculturalism and Anti-Racism Project

http://www.uua.org/re/youth/identity-formation/identity-based/btcp

Thrive: Leadership Schools for Youth and Young Adult of Color

http://www.uua.org/re/youth/events/multicultural-leadership-school

Books

A select list of books about people of color and Unitarian Universalism, authored or edited by Unitarian Universalists of color or featuring works by Unitarian Universalists of color

Turning Point: Essays on a New Unitarian Universalism edited by Frederic Muir (Skinner House Books, 2016)

Katha Sagar, Ocean of Stories: Hindu Wisdom for Every Age by Sarah Conover and Abhi Janamanchi (Skinner House Books, 2016)

Love Beyond God: Meditations by Adam Lawrence Dyer (Skinner House Books, 2016)

A Long Time Blooming: Meditations by Marta Valentín (Skinner House Books, 2014)

Falling into the Sky: A Meditation Anthology edited by Abhi Janamanchi and Abhimanyu Janamanchi (Skinner House Books, 2013)

Voices from the Margins edited by Jacqui James and Mark D. Morrison-Reed (Skinner House Books, 2012)

Darkening the Doorways: Black Trailblazers and Missed Opportunities in Unitarian Universalism by Mark D. Morrison-Reed (Skinner House Books, 2011)

The Arc of the Universe Is Long: Unitarian Universalists, Anti-Racism, and the Journey from Calgary by Leslie Takahashi-Morris, James (Chip) Roush, and Leon Spencer (Skinner House Books, 2009)

In Between: Memoir of an Integration Baby by Mark D. Morrison-Reed (Skinner House Books, 2008)

Soulwork: Anti-Racist Theologies in Dialogue edited by Marjorie Bowens-Wheatley and Nancy Palmer Jones (Skinner House Books, 2003)

Unitarian Universalism and the Quest for Racial Justice (Unitarian Universalist Association, 1994)

Black Pioneers in a White Denomination by Mark D. Morrison-Reed (Skinner House Books, 1992)

Been in the Storm So Long edited by Mark D. Morrison-Reed and Jacqui James (Skinner House Books, 1991)

Beyond the Critique of Racism: Moving Forward with Audacious Hope

Dr. Mark A. Hicks

Angus MacLean Professor of Religious
Education, mhicks@meadville.edu

Research on people of color in institutions of higher education suggests that people of color's participation in predominately white institutions can be counterproductive to their social, emotional, and intellectual development. William Smith calls this dynamic "racial battle fatigue," pointing to the long-term stress and anxiety that results from patterns of racial exclusion and exploitation. Being aware of this dynamic is important, but a single-minded focus on the dysfunctions and harm done by culturally white organizations also does a disservice to those outside its mainstream.

When the experience of cultural oppression unfolds in spiritual life, a healthy response must be more than naming and correcting the social wrong—pointing fingers at wrongdoers. Attention must be paid to how the trauma impacts personal visions about spiritual life, relationships of care with family and kinship groups, and how they collectively shape worldviews.

Faith communities, at their best, exist as locations for people to explore the big questions of life: how to love, trust, forgive, and reconcile more freely, how to be audaciously hopeful, creative, and engaged when a way forward seems impossible. Questions of racial oppression are particularly important locations for spiritual exploration, especially for people of color* whose lives are intertwined with racist structures that discount their humanity at every turn. Exploring how racism shapes a life is not linear, efficient work. It is messy, confusing, and often contradictory, co-opting participants into the systems they deplore. People who are targets of cultural oppression need intentional practices that nurture healthier ways of feeling and being.

Unitarian Universalist Spiritual Director Rev. Arvid Straube offers that good spiritual practices are generally practiced in the closet, in the living room, and then in the sanctuary. Closet practices are private and done with the goal of raising consciousness that leads to self-knowledge. Living-room practices are opportunities to explore insights and observations with a small, sympathetic group of people that affirm each other while figuring out complicated experiences. Sanctuary practices are places for sharing common visions that stretch across individual dispositions, values, and experiences. Such practices bear witness to everyone's humanity and encourage compassion, even when it's not fully clear why doing so is important.

People who are wounded by racism must explicitly seek ways to re-story themselves as whole human beings. They must find ways to clear away—even if only for moments at time—the toxic residue of racism in order to move toward wholeness. Most importantly, this work should not be done alone. Find ways to quiet your anxious head and heart. Invite people to a "living room" for sharing your experience. Align yourself with a spiritual community where your experiences can be valued, helping you to become ever more joyous and full-hearted in the skin you're in.

Following are questions that might help you unpack your experiences. There are many additional resources to call upon, but these may be a good place to begin. Each question can be enhanced by drilling into the specifics of personal experience: What was expected to happen and did not? What feelings did the experience evoke? What behaviors emerged over the course of the experience? How did other people respond to you? What kind of responses from other people would have made you feel better? Why?

Questions for Exploration

Questions for personal contemplation

Learning goal: What do you need to know about how you've lived your life?

- What experiences across your lifespan have blocked you from seeing yourself and living as a whole person?

- How have stories of pain and exclusion cut you off from the potential of richer relationships (such as in family, work, civic, and church life)?

- What practices have you adopted over time that serve to isolate and protect you from racial/ethnic stereotypes? When have those same practices served you well?

- How have you internalized negative generalizations about who you are? Who you should be? How do you pass those ideas on to others? Under what circumstances do you explicitly interrupt them?

- How has your experience as a person of color been a gift in your life?

- When have practices of resilience, compassion, empathy, hope, and interconnectedness served you well? Not so well?

Questions for small-group contemplation

Learning goal: What kind of positive opportunities can be created to lessen the trauma of racism in your life?

- How can the group help you normalize the contradictions and paradoxes inherently experienced as a person of color?

- Explore when you expected oppression to occur and it did not.

- Explore naming the kind of support that would affirm your sense of humanity in personal and congregational settings. Practice activities that show that support.

- How can the group help affirm the "intersections" of our lives (for example, you're more than your race, gender identity, sexual orientation, class, etc.)?

- Work to learn how other people are targeted for oppression—for example, Islamophobia, tensions between Africans, African Americans, Latinos(as), First Nation peoples, Asians/Pacific Islanders, immigrants, and second-generation peoples).

- Explore stories and experiences of bias within cultural groups that encourage oppression (for example, skin color, economic class, educational attainment, language usage, sexual orientation, etc.).

- How can the group help each member identify what thriving looks like in spiritual terms? How can the group love you into a bigger sense of self?

Questions for large-group/congregation-wide contemplation

Learning goal: How can the congregation normalize the practice of bearing witness to the spiritual pain experienced by people targeted for oppression?

- How could the congregation attend spiritually to youth targeted by police and/or teachers as troublemakers? How could it accompany people who experience discrimination on their jobs? How could it support parents and children who are in mixed-race families or are transracially adopted?

- What practices/programs might help people of color reconcile both the story they tell themselves about "who they are" as well as the story told by others as to "who they are"?

- How can the congregation normalize the positive contributions people of color make to the congregation? To the world (for example, using positive stories of people of color as examples of UU values)? Can people of color do more than teach about race/ethnicity?

- Instead of focusing only on the "problems" associated with managing a multiracial/multicultural community, highlight the positive contributions inherent in multicultural communities (for example, broader expressions of the sacred, diversity of thought, liturgy, religious education).

- Develop practices that "pay it forward." How can individuals and the congregation be rooted in a generous spirit of helping others grow around these ideas?

Buddhist practices remind us that healing comes when we let go of the pressures of perfection and allow room for grief, for relief, for misery, for joy. No one can ever fully escape the pains and disappointments we find in life. The good news is that we can create spiritual communities that make it a little more bearable.

References/Note

The relationship of racial identity attitudes to autonomy and mature interpersonal relationships is explored more fully by D. J. Taub and

M. K. McEwen in the *Journal of College Student Development*, 33(5): 439-46. Michael Smith explores the psychological impact of faculty of color on white campuses, in "Black faculty coping with racial battle fatigue: the campus racial climate in a post-civil rights era" in the book, *Conversations About Race by African American Faculty and Graduate Students* (New York: Peter Lang Press, 2004).

The term, "people of color" was created during the civil rights era as a way to describe the shared experience of people targeted for oppression because of their "race" and/or ethnicity. While recognizing the important distinctions within ethnic group, it is used here as shorthand for people of African descent, Caribbean, Native/American Indian, Asian and Pacific Islander, Latina(o) and Hispanic, Middle Eastern/Arab, and multiracial and multiethnic peoples.

About the Book

Contributors of this book are Unitarian Universalists of color of varying ages, ethnic backgrounds, and faith paths from around the United States. Panelists are three Unitarian Universalists ministers of color. Two Unitarian Universalist educators contributed Foreword, Afterword and an article for moving forward.